GW01606062

THE MYSTERIES OF ELEUSIS

The Secret Rites and Rituals of the Classical Greek Mystery Tradition

GOBLET D'ALVIELLA

Translated from the Dutch by Transcript

THE AQUARIAN PRESS
Wellingborough, Northamptonshire

Published in Holland as
Eleusinia: de mysteriën van Eleusis by W. N. Schors,
Amsterdam
First published in English 1981

British Library Cataloguing in Publication Data

D'Alviella, Goblet
The mysteries of Eleusis.
1. Eleusinian mysteries
I. Title
292'.3'8 BL795.E5

ISBN 0-85030-256-0

Typeset by Harper Phototypesetters, Northampton.
Printed in Great Britain by
Lowe and Brydone (Printers) Ltd., Thetford, Norfolk
and bound by Weatherby Woolnough,
Wellingborough, Northamptonshire.

CONTENTS

INTRODUCTION

This book does not aim to be a learned treatise, nor does it attempt to provide a comprehensive history of the Eleusinian Mysteries. As far as we know, the Mysteries encompassed ten centuries and like all institutions, they have, to some extent, been subjected to the law of change. Their conservatism was not due to them being particularly inaccessible to surrounding ideas, but rather to a willingness to accept new explanations, whilst retaining the old rites.

Initially, I will examine the development of the Mysteries during a period when respect for an oath, perhaps even fear of divine revenge, still guaranteed their secrecy, despite the fact that they were no longer protected by the severity of Athenian law. I will then re-examine the frequently discussed questions concerning their philosophical and moral significance, or at least establish some points of contact in the history of their relationship with the Great Mysteries of Greek philosophy. Finally, I will attempt to ascertain how they may have influenced the formation of the Christian liturgy which originated in a milieu imbued with Hellenic culture.

I fully realize the difficulty of my task. However, each of these problems has led, particularly in recent years, to so much profound study that now would seem the right moment to try to survey the subject as a whole.

Whilst archaeological discoveries have, so to speak, renewed the sources of our historical knowledge, a new science, comparative ethnography, also has a contribution to make to the interpretation of the general phenomena which characterized the earliest institutions and communities. By using both these approaches, we can draw important conclusions about the origins of these institutions.

I have therefore decided to divide the history of the Mysteries into seven consecutive stages.

1. In prehistoric times a group of Eleusinian families, devoted to the service of Demeter and Cora, practised magical rites to ensure the success of their harvest.

2. These *sacra gentilicia* were changed into Mysteries following the annexation of Eleusis by Athens. They include: (a) initiation, which was supposed to renew the life of the neophyte and which entailed transition to another world; (b) celebration of traditional rites, including mystical drama.

3. In the eighth century B.C., the 'rebirth' of the initiates was not only a condition of admittance to the Mysteries, but was the principal aim of their observance—and their value extended to the other side of the grave.

4. The division into Great and Small Mysteries signified a new step in the organization of the Eleusinian Mysteries.

5. Towards the end of the fifth century B.C. came Epoptism (the highest grade on initiation into the Eleusinian Mysteries) in place of the Great Mysteries. The doctrine of Orpheus, which had a firm hold in Eleusis at that time, certainly did not renounce its philosophical and moral pronouncements which constituted its nucleus. It furnished the initiates with a philosophy and ethics, whilst the ritual was, at the same time, extended in the spirit of the ceremonies which belonged to the worship of the mystical god Dionysus.

6. From the time of their blending with Orphean influence, up to their disappearance with the general collapse of paganism, the Mysteries reflected, in their view of deity and the life hereafter, Greek thought, which was based on a pantheistic philosophy.

7. In the meantime, Christendom itself adopted the form of the Mysteries, and the Eleusinian ceremonial was perpetuated in some of the rites of the victorious Church.

It should go without saying, that I will deal with this last problem in a strictly scientific way without entertaining any prejudice with regard to religious polemic. The conclusion concerning the origin of the forms which the Church uses for its doctrine remains separate from the question of whether this dogma is based on good grounds and even whether these forms best serve the intended purpose. When speaking about marriage ceremonies, Mgr Duchesne writes in his *Origines du Cults Chrétien*[1] that the entire Roman marriage ritual, apart from any specifically pagan aspects, such as foretelling the future from the intestines of animals and the sacrifices themselves, has been retained in the liturgy of the Church. This separation, he adds, is not isolated. The Church, which is very conservative in these matters, only changed aspects which were incompatible with its doctrine. I have already had the opportunity in another work of showing that, in this respect, the symbols followed the example of the rituals.[2] Indeed, apart from any sacramental significance they may have, rituals are nothing more than enacted symbols.

[1]Duchesne, *Origines du Culte Chrétien,* 2nd edn (Paris, 1898), p. 419.
[2]*De Wereldreis der Symbolen.*

CHAPTER 1
AN INITIATION IN ELEUSIS IN THE FIRST CENTURY A.D.

Athenian law punished by death both those who, from curiosity, unlawfully tried to penetrate the Mysteries of Eleusis, and those who indiscreetly passed them on to the profane. Historians testify that this precept was not merely a threat. But the secret was not so well guarded that one cannot find an occasional clue from behind the veil. Information gleaned from pagan writers, accusations levelled by the Church Fathers, a few memorials, which have survived the destruction of the old civilization, and finally the result of the excavations methodically carried out in modern times at Eleusis by archaeologists, have all inspired scholars such as Sainte-Croix, Lobeck, Guigniaut, Preller, Alfred maury, August Mommsen and especially, in the last ten years of the nineteenth century, François Lenormant and Paul Foucart, to attempt reconstructions which may be considered more or less accurate.

Using the information from their work, I would like to discuss, briefly, the effect of this institution. According to Cicero, it was the most fruitful of all the institutions created by Athens to raise the people from their crude barbarism to a highly civilized state.[1]

The Small Mysteries

The complete initiation into the Mysteries of Eleusis, during the time of their full development, consisted of three grades: the Small Mysteries, the Great Mysteries and Epoptism. Although these Mysteries in Athens were always a public institution, temporal power only interfered with their material administration. The priestly ceremonies were exclusively organized by two local families: the Eumolpides and the Kerykes, who held this office from the beginning of recorded history to the end of paganism. How many families today could even boast an ancestry spanning so many centuries?

It was necessary to have passed through the Small Mysteries before being granted admittance to the Great. The former were celebrated towards the end of winter, in the month of *anthesterion,* immediately after the Anthesteria or flower festivals which were established in honour of Demeter and Dionysus; the latter were celebrated in September, in the month of *boedromion,* between harvest and sowing-time. When people came from all over the Greek and Latin world to Eleusis for initiation, it became the custom to give a second enactment of the Small Mysteries at the end of the summer to spare the neophytes two consecutive journeys.[2] They went even further when Demetrius Poliorcetus, following his defeat of the armies of Ptolemy, asked the Athenians to initiate him into all three grades without any interval. It was in the middle of spring in the month of *munychion.* Because the Athenians did not dare to refuse the Macedonian king anything, a decree was issued establishing that this month would bear the names anthesterion and boedromion consecutively, after which a new decree would restore the calendar to normal.[3]

It is very strange that we have any information about the Small Mysteries. They were sometimes called the Mysteries of Agra because they were celebrated not in Eleusis but in Athens, in the suburb of Agra. Children and even foreigners (barbarians) were allowed admittance. It is said that they were set up so as to extend the prerogative of initiation to Hercules, who was excluded from the Great Mysteries because he was a foreigner.

There seems to be an allusion to these ceremonies on a painted vase which portrays the son of Alcmena in the company of the Eleusinian gods. Demeter is sitting in the middle with a calathus on her head; Aphrodite is sitting on her right hand side and Eros at her feet. On her left is Persephone holding a torch in her hand, while the young Iacchus is wielding a horn of plenty. Behind these gods, a priest, dressed in a short Thracian tunic, is waving two torches. In the background Triptolemus can be seen on his chariot, between Dionysus who is holding a thyrsus and Hercules, armed with his club. A woman, sitting in the foreground in a meditative pose, is perhaps a candidate.[4]

This illustration does not give us any information about the initiation episodes. It merely shows us the principal characters involved and appears to be connected with a nocturnal ceremony. All that we learn from short allusions by certain classical writers is that the Small Mysteries consisted, above all, of sacrifices and purifications, notably a purification ceremony in the Illissos, and that they were related to the worship of Dionysus and Demeter.[5]

Various monuments show us how this purification took place. The neophyte, with his clothes removed, placed his left foot on the body of a dead sacrificial animal—usually a ram—and purifying water was poured over his head.[6] Or, he sat down on a seat, with his head covered by a heavy veil, and a priestess would fan him with a kind of bellows: the mystical fan.[7]

According to Clement of Alexandria, the neophytes received instruction in the Small Mysteries which prepared them for the Great Mysteries.[8] From that moment on, they bore the title of 'mystai'.

Preparations for the Great Mysteries

The Great Mysteries began on the thirteenth day of boedromion with the young men leaving for Eleusis on the orders of their *kosmétes* to fetch the *hiera* or sacred objects which were entrusted to the care of the high priest (ὁ ἱεϱὰ φαίνων, 'he who shows the sacred objects'). They returned the following day, accompanied by the high priest, bringing the *hiera* along in a cart. When the procession approached Athens, the people went to meet it at the bridge of the Athenian Cephissus, wearing masks. Between both groups there was an exchange of abusive language and rude jokes, known as *nephyrismos,* after passing the sanctuary which the Gephyreans owned in the neighbourhood.

It is possible that the *gephyrismos* contributed as much to the formation of Attic comedy as to the masquerades of the Dionysian Hellenes.[9] The sacred objects were then laid down in a sanctuary, built under the Acropolis, and bearing the name 'Eleusinion'.[10]

On the fifteenth day of the month, the neophytes of both sexes gathered at the gate of Poecile, each group under the leadership of a member of the Eumolpides or the Kerykes who acted as their initiator. They would be overexcited by the expectation of the revelations. People would scream, even jostle each other in spite of the attempts of the Kerykes, under the leadership of the archon-king, to keep order at the assembly. One should not forget that the servants of the Bacchanalia took part in the celebration and that orgies often went hand in hand with devotion.

But then the priests would arrive and, at a nod from the high priest, the uproar would be replaced by a devoted silence.[11]

The high priest was a Eumolpide of mature age and great experience, who was not only required to have a perfect knowledge of the rites but also, as the name 'Eu-mol-pos' ('he who sings well') indicates, a sufficiently flexible voice to be able to render the songs to both goddesses in the tone desired. Next to him stood the torch-bearer, the Daduchus (*δαοῦχος*) who arranges with him the special features of the initiation. Both wore a purple cloak and were crowned with myrtle; they also bore the diadem which was taken at the battle of Marathon by the Persian soldiers as a mark of royal distinction. So great was the sanctity of these people that, in the last centuries of the Mysteries, one was not allowed to call them by their own name. They were simply the Hierophant and the Daduchus.

Next came the two high priestesses who attended to the candidate of their sex, probably with the priestess of Demeter;[12] the sacred herald (Keryx), a kind of master of ceremonies who arranged the movements of the candidates; the Epibomios, whose task consisted of preparing the altars; and finally a whole series of subordinate priests who all had their own distinguishing marks and specific functions.

'Is there anyone present whose hands are not clean? Is there anyone with a voice which cannot be understood?[13] Is there anyone who is guilty of murder or sacrilege or who has surrendered to black magic? Let him withdraw!' Following this opening speech by the high priest of the Great Mysteries, there was undoubtedly a short pause; the Hierophant or the Daduchus then explained the programme of the ceremony and emphasized the formalities which the neophytes had to fulfil. Each initiator explained these regulations to the neophytes in his group. These people had to prove that they had been initiated into the Small Mysteries and had remitted the initiation fees to the priests; they had to swear to keep the secret, to observe certain fasts and also to abstain throughout the ceremonies from any forbidden food such as beans, pomegranates and even fish.

On the day of the 16th, the Mystics would set out for the seashore, clothed only in a deer skin. Each one would bring the piglet which he would subsequently sacrifice to Demeter. The ceremony is led by *hydranoi* or purification priests. Suddenly the cry, 'Into the sea, Mystics!' (Αλαδε μύσται) would reverbrate across the shore. The latter would dive madly into the briny waves without letting go of their four-legged companions, who, undoubtedly, would be less enthusiastic![14] In the afternoon an expiatory sacrifice is celebrated in the Eleusinion, called 'soterion' the deliverer during which Demeter is invoked for the Boulè and for the people. Each Mystic then sacrifices his piglet on small, temporary altars set up within the enclosure of the sanctuary. When the victim has been killed and roasted, the thigh bones are burnt in honour of Demeter; the rest is taken away and eaten by the donor![15] It should not, therefore, cause surprise when one of Aristophanes' characters, Xanthias, in *The Frogs* says 'Oh, sublime and revered daughter of Demeter, what a wonderful smell of roast pork![16]

On the seventeenth day, the Mystics bring floral tributes to Dionysus and, when evening has fallen, they take part in a wake in honour of Asclepios, the god of healing in Epidaurus. On the morning of the eighteenth, everyone again assembles before the Eleusinion in order to carry the statues of both goddesses to the temple of Asclepios where the Epidaurean celebrations will take place. An abridged repetition of the preceding ceremonies then took place for the benefit of the latecomers who could not be present at the opening of the celebrations.

According to custom, the Greeks explained this practice by the following myth: when Asclepios wanted to be initiated, he arrived too late, and the Epidaurians were established so that it would not be necessary to repeat all the preparations for the initiation. I should like to draw attention to the fact that Asclepios descended into the Underworld like Persephone and Dionysus. On these grounds, it is not surprising that he is included among the Eleusinian gods.

The Procession of Eleusis

The pilgrim's departure for Eleusis took place on the nineteenth day. The procession was formed in front of the Eleusinion, or, during the Empire, in the Pompeion, where, according to Pausanias, the main religious processions were formed.[17] It was headed by the Iacchagogos, the leader of Iacchus, in front of the statue of the young gold. Iacchus, represented as a child, crowned with myrtle and holding a torch in his hand, originally seems to have been a local tutelary spirit—according to Strabo, 'a demon or servant of Demeter'[18]—who was later fused with the child, Dionysus. The Orphian blending of systems connected him with Dionysus Zagreus, the legend of whom was celebrated by the Cretans, a legend which would go down well in an era when some cannibalism was practised. As the son of Zeus and Demeter, he was lured by means of toys into a trap by the Titans, instigated by the jealousy of Hera. These monsters killed him, hacked him to pieces and ate him, except for the heart, which Pallas brought to Zeus. The latter brought the child back to life and then crushed the murderers.[19] Next to the god, there would be two priestesses, one of whom represented his nurse. Several priests carried bags made of valuable cloth containing his traditional toys, described to us by Clement of Alexandria: knucklebones, a ball, an apple, a mirror, a top and a doll.[20] Other sacred objects were enclosed in bladders tied with purple ribbons. Then came a cart, drawn by four white horses and carrying the tall calathus basket which contained sheaves of corn.

The remaining first-fruits of the harvest, which had to be supplied by not only the inhabitants of Attica, but by all people ruled by Athens, are arranged in pots and borne on the heads of the Kernophores, priestesses dressed in white.

Then comes the Hieraules or head of the sacred music, who, while playing on the flute, would conduct a line of *hymnodï* and *hymnêtiai.* Choruses, performed in honour of Iacchus, were reproduced or imitated by Aristophanes in his comedy, *The Frogs:*

> Iacchus, most honoured god, come quickly to our voice. . . . Wave the burning torches and fan their glow, Iacchus, O Iacchus, brilliant star of the nocturnal mysteries. The meadow land sparkles with a thousand fires; the old men throw off the weight of care and long years; they are again untiring in their participation in your sacred choruses, and you, O blessed one, with a torch in your hand, leading the dances of youth to this moist carpet of flowers.[21]

According to a passage in Sophocles, the images of Dionysus, Demeter and Persephone—or rather Cora, as this goddess is called in Eleusinian tradition—also figured in the procession.[22] Behind followed the sacrificial animals, crowded together. Finally, at the end of the procession, came the Mystics with a large proportion of the Athenian population, carrying torches in their hands.[23]

The long procession, which had about twenty kilometres to cover, always left Athens by the Dipylon gate. Led by the Epheboi, who were armed with a shield and a lance and wore the white *chlamys* which they had received through the generosity of Herodes Atticus,[24] they followed the road to Eleusis, making shorter or longer stops at some of the many chapels which gave this road its sacred name.

The procession followed approximately the same road which nowadays leads to the village of Lefsina, the humble descendant of the former Eleusis. There were numerous monuments, particularly along the first part of the road. These were memorial temples, dedicated to the memory of the true or legendary heroes, soothsayers, envoys, artists, famous women and even a *demi-mondaine,* Pythonice. Her lover, Harpalos, a lieutenant of Alexander, who had stayed behind in Greece to guard his master's treasure, had ordered this tomb to be erected at the highest point along the road, although, if we are to believe Plutarch, it was more costly than it was beautiful. There were also various sanctuaries intended to keep alive the memory of the adventures and exploits or the charity of the gods. For example, the temple which was dedicated jointly to the goddesses Demeter, Cora, Poseidon and Athene, was erected close to the spot where Phytalos planted the first fig tree, a gift from the goddess who was seeking her daughter, and the little temple of the Indulgent Zeus (Μειλιχίος) is on the spot where Theseus went to be purified because he had killed the robbers who tormented Attica, among them his kinsman Sinis. People would be dancing everywhere in honour of the local deity; *dithyrambs* and *paeans* would be intoned and sacrifices and libations performed.

The procession then crossed the Cephisus over the bridge which was the scene of the *gephyrismos,* leaving behind the olive grove which still exists today and where, according to Sophocles 'numerous nightingales in cool valleys spread their harmonious complaint beneath the thick foliage of the forest, impervious to sun rays and winter wind alike, where the revelling Dionysus walks, surrounded by his nurse-goddesses.'[25]

After the bare steppes came shady woods and rich arable land. The procession then climbed the slopes of the mountain, Corydallos, the advance sentry of the Parnes, which closes this part of the bay of Athens. In the east, across the sombre green of the olive trees, the snow-white marble of the Parthenon, tinted pink by the last rays of the sun, would be complemented by the purple background of the Hymettus mountains. But before long, this fairy-like spectacle would reach the barren pass where the cloister of Daphne replaced the temple of Apollo. At this point the sanctuary of Aphrodite rises up on the other side of the pass; then the road slopes down towards the seashore. Here the procession turned right, following the bank of the bay of Eleusis. In this way they reached the two ponds filled with brackish water, the Rheitoi, one dedicated to Cora, the other to Demeter. The Mystics would stop here for further purification. As soon as they had crossed the old boundary of the kingdom of Eleusis, they would meet the representatives of an old local family, the Croconides or descendants of the legendary Crocon, who tied yellow ribbons on their left wrists and right ankles to protect them against the evil eye. They would then cross the Eleusinian Cephisus at a place called Erineos where, according to tradition, the abduction of Cora took place, close to the Rarian Field where the first harvest of Attica grew.

When evening had fallen, brilliantly lit the sacred buildings of Eleusis would stand out in flaming lines against the night horizon. The excitement would continue to increase, perhaps stimulated further by the numerous libations after nightfall in honour of the wine-god.[26] Eventually, the enthusiasm would become almost frenzied—the Mystics, swaying with their torches or dancing exuberantly to the sound of the cymbals. Finally, with a thousand-fold cry, 'Iacchus! O Iacchus!', the multitude would disappear within the walls of Eleusis by the flickering light of the two gigantic pitch-pots, burning in front of the temple of Triptolemus.[27] It was one of those scenes of barbaric splendour and frenized ecstasy which can still be found in Jagernath, Benares, Candy and Bangkok amongst the remnants of the ancient Eastern religions.[28]

This is where the public part of the ceremonies ended. Only the procession of priests crossed the threshold of the double enclosure of the sanctuary where the high priest set down the sacred objects in the megaron. The Mystics would find lodgings in the town unless, as in Olympia, they slept in tents of leaves or in temporary barracks. In the mild autumn of Attica, of course, this was not particularly important.

The Sacred Evenings

On the twentieth day, the neophytes left for the portals which formed the main entrance to the Eleusinion, to attend the solemn sacrifice to the gods.

A certain number of goats, rams, pigs and oxen were killed on the high altar which bore a frieze depicting the principal Eleusinion symbols.[29] Corn, barley and biscuits made from cereals from the Rarian Field were also offered to Demeter.

That same evening the sacred wakes or Mystical Nights began.[30] There were probably three of them. Although no one is able to give an accurate description, the principal episodes have been successfully discovered: the transfer of the symbols; the visit to the Underworld; the enactment of mystical drama.

On one of the evenings, the Mystics went with torches to look for Cora in the sacred places which represented the stations of the suffering of Demeter. Some of the sacred places, like Erineos, lay in the nearby town. Others lay at the Propylaea, such as the well of Callichorus, where the local women sang the first chorus in honour of Demeter;[31] or within the enclosure, such as the Stone of Sorrow where the goddess was said to sit when she was weary and disheartened. It was the evening which Fulgen calls the *dies lampadorum,* the first of the sacred wakes.

The transfer of the sacred objects, the παραδόσις τῶν ἱερῶν, took place in front of the megaron where only the high priest might enter. This holiest of holy places certainly formed a kind of retreat, closed off in the telesterion or initiation palace. The wide-open doors allowed the symbols to be seen, illuminated by a strong light. Perhaps the initiates filed past the entrance; but it is also possible that this display took place on one of the following evenings for the benefit of the Mystics who had assembled in the inner court, or even at the end of the procedures. A vase in the museum at Naples shows candidates sitting under the trees of the sacred enclosure. A priest, or mystagogue, is handing them a chalice which he is filling from a leather bag. Near him, on the ground, is a bag of biscuits. This kind of communion, in which the Mystics broke their fast, was a rememberance of the offering of the cyceon to Demeter. It ended with the communication of the formula which must serve as a password for the candidate for the Great Mysteries: 'I have fasted, I have drunk cyceon; I have taken from the bladder, and after taking from the bladder I have laid it in the calathus; I have taken it again from the calathus and placed it again in the bladder.'

The actual proceedings took place in the telesterion.[32] This building, one of the most vast in the whole of Greece, was a cross between a temple and a theatre. Situated against the rocks of the Acropolis, it covered an area of more than 2,700 square metres and could hold about three thousand spectators. The centre section was used as an amphitheatre where eight rows of steps encircled the stage. The roof, which let in the light through a wide opening, was supported by seven parallel rows of six pillars. Besides the two entrance doors, which opened on to the colonnade, there were two passages on either side, undoubtedly to facilitate the entrance or exit of the players.[33]

The priests and priestesses formed the members of the troupe. We know that in the days of Porphyros, the high priest played the role of the Demiourgos, the organizer of the Universe; the Daduchus played Helios; the Epibomios took the part of Selene; the Keryx, that of Hermes, the leader of souls.[34] Demeter was represented by her priestess.[35] There were also characters of more than natural size, monsters and various kinds of fantastic beings. Plato says that the apparitions in the Elysian Fields would excel even those of Eleusis which were perfect, clear and immutable.[36] François Lenormant wittily concludes from this that they took place in semi-obscurity, that they were difficult to understand and soon disappeared.[37]

The performances took up the second and third of the sacred evenings, probably the twenty-second and twenty-third day.[38] One of them was devoted to the performances of the legend of Demeter— to 'mystical drama', according to the expression of Clement of Alexandria—the other to the visit to the Underworld and the Elysian Fields.

The Visit to the Other World

At the moment of death, writes Plutarch, the spirit receives an impression which is very similar to that experienced at initiation into the Mysteries. It is first a passage through the unknown, with difficult circuitous routes in the dark, along an endless road. Before the end is reached, fear is at its peak, one trembles, one shivers with fear, a cold sweat breaks out all over. But then suddenly a wonderful light appears before one's eyes; one is transported to delightful places and meadows where song and dance fill the air, where one hears sacred words and witnesses mystical appearances.[39]

When, in 1814, English archaeologists made the first excavations in the ruins of Eleusis, they believed that they had discovered the traces of a large, underground vault under the telesterion. They hastened to conclude that it had served to represent the Underworld. When later investigations disproved the existence of this subterranean area, the scholars changed their minds and many of them were inclined to dispute the candidates' wandering through the realm of Hades. However, I think this scepticism is too severe. Within the vast area of the Eleusinion there may have been many parts which now no longer exist. At the time of the first international exhibition in Paris, visitors who went into the cellars beneath the attractions of the Trocadero, found panoramas which introduced them to the mines, the wonders of the subterranean world and the horrors of prehistoric times. There were long, winding passages, which led, at intervals, to areas which were so cleverly arranged that they gave the illusion of perspective. What will be left of these layouts in fifteen or sixteen centuries time? Indeed, what is left now, after only a few years?[40]

I therefore believe that there is no serious reason to reject the evidence of classical tradition. It is likely that the candidates, crowned with myrtle as shown on certain monuments, carrying a *bacchos* or thyrsus, peculiar to the Eleusinian Mysteries, followed the torch of their mystagogue in the dark galleries, the walls of which were here and there broken through to reveal, in an ominous light, first the throne and court of Hades and then the torture of criminals, sentenced to receive their punishment here.

They were then brought before the telesterion and soon would see a strong light streaming through the opening in the room, while strange noises and melodious music would arise from within. Suddenly the doors would fly open, the veils fall away and, completely blinded by a bright light, which texts and descriptions unanimously call the 'splendour', the Mystics were led in solemn silence to the steps of the amphitheatre, their eyes fixed on the radiant visions of the divine world, succeeding each other on the stage.[41]

They not only saw the great deities of Eleusis, but also the shades of the Blessed dressed in white, roaming through blooming meadows, led by choruses singing Orphean songs. 'Eleusis', says Isocrates 'is a sanctuary for the common good of the whole earth, and of all the sacred matters known to man it is the one which awakens the most fear and gives the most peace'.

Which of us, on seeing a performance of Gluck's *Orpheus* for the first time, has been able to resist the somewhat melancholy, infinitely gentle, yet penetrating impression which emanates not only from the maestro's sweet melodies, but also from the shades filing past, talking amongst each other in the woods of painted backcloth, behind a gauze veil, in a bluish light, as dim as pale azure? How much stronger and more lasting this impression must be when the spectator believes he is witnessing a true picture of his final destiny.

It is there, writes Plutarch, that a man, whose initiation has made him perfect, liberated and truly master of himself, speaks with righteous and pure spirits, and sees with disdain the impure multitude of the profane and uninitiated sinking deeper into the mud and impenetrable darkness.[42] Foucart, who does not accept the explanation of the consecutive visits to the Underworld and the Elysian Fields, has put forward a supposition which also concurs with the circumstances of these performances. He suggests that, for want of a vault, the telesterion was divided into two floors. The seven parallel rows of pillars, the existence of which has been established, divided the lower floor into sections, each of which was devoted to a part of the Underworld. When the Mystics had walked far enough around, they were brought to the upper storey by means of the other flight of steps which led on to the platform of the cliff against which the building stood. From there they went into the upper chamber on the same floor where the representation of the Elysian Fields was arranged and where the *hiera* were exhibited.[43]

Perhaps further discoveries will shed light on the question. In any case, it is certain that there were apparitions and stage effects which suggest a rather complex mechanism. Does not Plato compare the beholding of the Ideas by the disembodied spirits with the shades which are revealed in the Mysteries?[44]

Mystical Drama

Mystical drama forms the best known part of the Greek mysteries, precisely because there was nothing secretive about the subject matter which had been public knowledge to writers of myths since time immemorial. The setting, determined by tradition, has undoubtedly remained as good as unchanged throughout the ages. It is easy to reconstruct this with the help of the Homeric Hymn in honour of Demeter, dating from the end of the eighth or the beginning of the seventh century B.C. The ending of this Hymn establishes that it was written for the Mysteries and tells of the attitude of the goddess herself:

> Happy are the mortals who have been able to behold these great enactments. But he who is not initiated, who has not taken part in these great ceremonies, is forever deprived of his fate, which awaits the former, when death has carried him to the places of darkness.[45]

The first act takes place in a mythical region, Nysa, not far from Eleusis. The young Cora is frolicking with her playmate in meadows of blooming violets, irisses, saffron and hyacinths. Her attention is suddenly drawn to an even more beautiful flower: the narcissus. Hardly has she plucked it before Hades rushes out of a cave on his golden chariot. He seizes the divine maiden, in spite of her struggles, and takes her with him to the Underworld.

Demeter hears her daughter's cries. She hastens after her; but only the rumbling of thunder, bronze beaten by a priest in the wings,[46] answers the cries of the dispairing mother. For nine days and nine nights she scours the land, with a torch in her hand, and without eating any food. During her searches she meets Hecate who saw the abduction but did not recognize the abductor; then Helios accuses Pluto but observes that he acted with the consent of Zeus. On hearing this, Demeter tears her clothes and, after assuming the appearance of a poor, old woman, sets out for the town of Eleusis.

In the next act the goddess is sitting on the Stone of Sorrow by the well where the daughters of King Celeos come and draw the water for the royal household. It is known that drawing water and milking cows in early times was the special occupation of the young princesses. When questioned by a daughter of Celeos, she tells her that she is called Deo; that she was captured by robbers on Crete; that she has escaped from their hands and is seeking a post, either as a governess, or as a housekeeper or even a nursery maid. After requesting permission from their mother, the princesses take their protégée back to the palace to look after their small brother Demophoon. But Deo still grieves. She refuses all food until, a little cheered by the ultra-naturalistic jokes of a servant girl, she takes a drink made of water, flour, honey and mint: this is the famous cyceon. Then follow several occurrences in the place where the goddess is living, ending with her revealing her identity. Celeos offers her hospitality in a temple which he builds for her.

The third act takes place in the temple. The goddess is still inconsolable and her mourning affects the whole of nature which becomes infertile. In vain the principal gods come and beseech Demeter, one by one, to return to Olympus. She persists in her resolution to maintain her withdrawal as long as her daughter is not returned to her. Consternation prevails amongst the people and penetrates the abode of the immortals.

Meanwhile Zeus, who is very embarrassed about the situation, sends Hermes to Pluto to persuade him to return Cora. The king of Hades does not dare to refuse and before long Cora is brought into daylight again by Hermes and hastens to the temple of Eleusis to embrace her mother.

After the first outpourings, Demeter asks her anxiously if she has eaten any food in Hades. Cora admits that on leaving she accepted a pomegranate seed from her husband. It appears that, because of this, her return to the light cannot be permanent. But Zeus again acts as intermediary, to effect an agreement. Demeter herself informs her daughter that this year she must spend the winter with her husband: 'When the fragrant spring bedecks the earth with a thousand flowers, you will ascend from your sombre abode through a miracle which is as great for the gods as it is for man.'[47]

Rhea then comes to fetch both goddesses to guide them back to Olympus. But Demeter first wishes to express her thanks to Celeos by establishing the Mysteries, the guardianship of which is entrusted to him with the order to pass it on to his descendants.

The play ends with a kind of apotheosis.[48] Triptolemus sits in a chariot drawn by snakes while holding in his hand the ears of corn given to him by Demeter with instructions to spread the knowledge of agriculture amongst all people. Three times Hecate arises from the earth. The young Iacchus appears, wreathed in ivy. Finally, both goddesses ascend to the abode of the gods, welcomed by the whole of Olympus.

One cannot say with certainty that the performance of the play of

Demeter was preceded by that of the journeys introduced later. M. W. Ramsay is of the opinion that since mystical drama is probably the oldest part of the Mysteries, it probably took precedence over later additions.[49]

However, as I shall show later, the visit to the other world probably recalls the initiation which enabled the profane to participate in the *sacra,* which includes the mystical drama. Thus, it would seem more logical to suppose that, initially at least, this drama took second place on the programme.

The days between the Sacred Evenings were intended as a period of rest, unless the neophytes used their free time to visit the temples in the town, the sanctuaries of Triptolemus, of Zeus, Eubouleus, Poseidon Pater, Demeter, the Propylaea, etc.

Epoptism—the Highest Initiation

The Great Mysteries were followed by Epoptism. 'There are', writes Seneca, 'religious mysteries which cannot be revealed in one day. Eleusis keeps secrets in store for those who come and visit her again.'[50] According to Plutarch, following initiation into the Great Mysteries, the earliest one could be allowed into Epoptism was one year later.[51] But the exceptions were undoubtedly increasingly numerous.

Once again, writers cannot agree here concerning the day of the ceremony. If, however, the telesterion was used for the performances of the Great Mysteries on the evenings of the twenty-second and the twenty-third, the conferment of the highest degree would, of necessity, take place on the twenty-fourth.[52] The Mystics who desired this highest degree, had to submit their claims to the Daduchus. They received a medal, inscribed with symbols connected with the Mysteries, i.e. the head of Demeter or an ear of corn and a poppy with the word ἐπόψ. Several of these medals have been discovered in the area around Eleusis.[53] Epoptism likewise consisted of performances.

One of the principal characters was Dionysus, particularly in the form of Zagreus. First of all there was an enactment of the hierogamy (sacred marriage) of Zeus and Demeter.[54] The main parts were played by the high priest and priestess of Demeter. At a given moment, a brilliant light spread over the scene and a solemn voice would call out from a gloomy cave, where the god had taken the goddess: 'The venerable goddess has brought the sacred child into the world. Brimo [the strong] has borne Brimos [the strong].'[55] Then Zagreus appeared represented, in accordance with Cretan tradition, by a child with the head of a bull, attended by nymphs and the Curetes. It would seem from the evidence of Clement of Alexandria that the passion of Zagreus was enacted with full details.[56] The Titans took possession of the child and pretended to kill him and tear him into pieces. If we are to believe some writers, Zagreus was represented by a bull, from which the participants tore off pieces of flesh and swallowed it raw.

I find it difficult to believe, however, that this 'shouldering', which was certainly applied in the Dionysian *thiasoi,* could have been an integral, official part of the Eleusinian form of worship. It is possible that they were content to kill a bull and simply simulate the rest.

Zeus revenged the death of his son by crushing the Titans to pieces after which the Curetes gathered the torn limbs of the young god together so as to bury him solemnly on Parnassus. But before long, Dionysus returned to life again—in the shape of the handsome young man, rendered immortal by sculpture in the Alexandrian era. Joy followed sorrow and the candidates took part in this expression of joy in honour of the god who had arisen from the dead; finally the Hierophant showed them an ear of wheat, as the highest and most perfect symbol of the initiation.[57]

Perhaps this ear, which the high priest silently reaped, sprang from the grave of Zagreus himself, a symbol which may have been borrowed from Egyptian symbolism where some monuments show plants or ears of corn sprouting from the sarcophagus of Osiris.[58]

It is evident that the conferment of this degree also included the communication of symbols and formulas, if not dogma. On various decorated relics believed to be connected with this degree, one can see the neophyte, recognizable by the deerskin which he wears over his shoulders, stroking the tame snake which is poised on the lap of Demeter.[59] The sentence whereby the Epopts recognized each other differs somewhat from the formula used for the previous initiation. The words of this sentence have also been handed down to us by Clement of Alexandria: 'I have eaten from the *tympanon,* I have drunk from the *kymbalon,* I have carried the *kernos* [the fan] and I have crawled under the *pastos* [bridal-bed].'[60]

Could there have been a fourth degree of initiation as Sir F. J. F. Marchal suggested in an account published in 1851?[61] I should like to observe here that before the Hierophant and the Daduchus assumed their functions, they had to submit to a kind of priest-initiation which Theon of Smyrna called the end of Epoptism (τέλος της ἐποπτείας).[62]

Theodoret for his part says, 'None of them knows what the Hierophant knows. The majority only see what is presented; the priests perform the rites of the Mysteries but only the high priest knows the reasons for what he is doing and he communicates this information to whoever he thinks fit.'[63]

According to Foucart, this only applies to the Mysteries of Lampsacus (Lepsek). In Eleusis, investiture with the office of Hierophant would only have been a simple ceremony, preceded by an examination (δοκιμασία) with the aim of ascertaining if the office-bearer had all the requisite abilities to carry out his function. Like the Daduchus, he certainly had to have special knowledge, both occult and profane; but this was of a ritual kind and formed the sacred tradition, τὰ πάτρια of the Eumolpides and the Kerykes.

The Sequel to the Mysteries

The Mystics who were not aspiring to Epoptism could naturally return home after the twenty-fifth, perhaps after a ceremony which represented the farewell of Demeter and Cora, when the latter went to visit her husband for a while.[64] But the majority preferred to remain in Eleusis to attend the public festivities with which the Mysteries were brought to a close. They included wrestling, music and theatrical competitions as well as horse-racing. These games are considered to be the oldest in Greece. The main prize consisted of a measure of barley, harvested from the Rarian Field. There were also theatrical performances, usually tragedies of a religious nature, performed by the company of Dionysian actors, the *Dionysiacoi Technitai,* in the theatre on the slope of the Eleusinian Acropolis.[65] This singular guild—which calls to mind the Societies of Rhetoricians and, in general, the dramatic groups which performed mystery plays at religious ceremonies in the Middle Ages—held certain privileges in Eleusis and, in particular, had the use of a chapel within the enclosure of the Eleusinion.

Whilst they were originally celebrated every five years and only lasted one day, the Eleusinian games underwent a major expansion during the period of the Empire. Among the entertainments which formed the public conclusion of the Mysteries was also a mock fight with stones. This stone-throwing perhaps had the aim of justifying the prediction of the Homeric Hymn attributed to Demeter, that one day her worshippers would fight each other violently, unless the prediction was invented in order to explain the custom and that this—like the *gephyrismos*—was an allusion to the ancient disputes between Eleusis and Athens. A final religious ceremony took place on the departure of the Mystics. The priests charged with purification filled two *plenochoes* with water; they were two pots shaped like tureens, one of which was placed in the east, the other in the west, while the priests invoked the gods of life and death respectively; they then threw the contents on the earth, while reciting the following formula: 'ὕε, κύε, ὑπερκιέ', i.e. 'Make fertile, bring forth, bring forth to the utmost'.[66]

There can be no doubt as to the purpose of this rite. Pouring water on the ground or dipping a sacred object in liquid is one of the most widespread ritual methods of bringing about rainfall. In their description of the Mysteries of the Tuysayans of North America, J. W. Fewkes and A. M. Stephens state that, on the first day of the celebration, stalks are planted in pots filled with sand and then generously sprinkled so as to ensure rainfall on the sown fields.[67] During the feast of the Tabernacle, the Jews used to draw water from the fountain of Siloe and then poured it amidst the blast of trumpets over the altar of the Temple. According to a rabbinical tradition, stated by Robertson Smith,[68] the purpose of this rite was to ensure rain throughout the following year.

Here in Eleusis, therefore, we undoubtedly have the remains of an ancient magical act which has become a tribute to the powers of fertility of the two goddesses and which has, in turn, been confused with the power of fertility of nature. It is, in a way, the whole history of the Mysteries.

[1]*De Legibus,* lib. II, ch. 14.

[2]'Εφήμερις ἀρχαιολογική, a journal of the Archaeological Society of Athens (1887), p. 185.

[3]Plutarch, *Vita Demetrii,* part I, ch. 26.

[4]Reproduced by Lenormant in the *Dictionnaire de Daremberg et Saglio,* part II, fig. 2630. The initiation of Heracles is also illustrated on a Greek measure in the museum in Brussels (Catal. Somzée collection, No. 45).

[5]Etienne de Byzance says that the Small Mysteries are a representation of the life of Dionysus.

[6]Bon de Witte, 'L'Expiation de Thésée in the *Gazette Archéologique* (1884), part IX, p. 353.

[7]Lovatelli, 'Un Vasos Cinerario', in the *Bullet. della Commis. Arch. Commun.* 1897, pl. 2-3.

[8]*Stromata,* Book 5, p. 689, (Potter).

[9]According to Aug. Mommsen, this scene took place on the fifteenth day of boedromion when the great procession set out for Athens (*Feste der Stadt Athen,* p. 227, note 3). According to Lenormant, it took place on the return of the initiates, after the initiation. Foucart has put forward strong reasons for its coinciding with the arrival of the *hiera* (*Recherches sur les Mystères d'Eleusis,* 2nd account, p. 105).

[10]The learned expounder of Pausanias, M. G. Frazer, suggests the possibility that the Eleusinion of Athens could well have been an area which held the temples of Demeter, Cora and Triptolemus. *Pausanias,* (London, 1898), part III, p. 119.

[11]Plutarch, *De profectibus in virtute,* ed. Didot, p. 97.

[12]It is most probably this priestess who is depicted in the central motif of an elegant cyclix with a black background and red figures. This cyclix—probably fifteenth century—is part of the Hirsch collection (but I believe as yet unissued) in the Royal numismatic cabinet in Brussels. On the fine, graceful head is a wreath of flowers which appears to be a derivation of the calathus, in her right hand she is holding, above an altar, three long ears of corn lying side by side. Next to this scene the word *Δημητϱος* [*ιεϱεια*] is painted. Foucart gives interesting information (2nd report, pp. 68-71) about this priestess who was the equivalent of a high priest and perhaps represented an older form of Eleusinian devotion in which Demeter was simply worshipped as the patroness of agriculture. Appointed for life, she was only referred to by her title.

Some celebrations in honour of the goddesses were led by her alone and around 378 B.C. the high priest Callias was convicted by the Hellenic court, accused of ungodliness because he had taken the liberty of killing a sacrificial animal, the slaughter of which was the right of the priestess.

[13] *Ὅστις φωνὴν ἀξύνετος* Libanius contends that this exclusion related to those who could not speak Greek (*Orationes,* Κοϱινθιων λογος, (Reiske), part IV, p. 356). According to Foucart, it related to those who, on account of some physical disability, would be unable to repeat the initiation formulas with the prescribed intonation (*Recherches sur l'origine et la nature des Mystères d'Eleusis,* first account (Paris, 1895), p. 33).

[14]During this procedure, Mystics were sometimes dragged away or maimed by sharks. This was naturally seen as a bad omen.

[15]A bas-relief, originally from Eleusis, shows a family sacrificing a pig to the great goddesses. (Panofka, *Antiquités du Cabinet Pourtalès.*) pl. 18.

[16]Aristophanes, *Ranae* (Didot), line 338.

[17]Pausanias 1, 2, 4.

[18]Strabo, *Geography,* ch. 3 (Didot), p. 402.

[19]Decharme, *Mythologie de la Grèce antique* (Paris, 1886), p. 468.

[20]*Protreptique II,* (Potter), p. 15.

[21]Aristophanes, *Ranae,* line 324 and following (Didot).

[22]Sophocles, *Leconte de Lisle,* (Paris, 1877), p. 179.

[23]A bas-relief found in Eleusis and printed by Spon in the second part of his *Voyage d'Italie et du Levant* shows a long line of Mystics marching past, carrying torches. (Lyon, 1678), part II, p. 283.

[24]Philostates, *Vitae Sophistarum* II, 1, 8 (Westermann), p. 227.
[25]Sophocles, *Leconte de Lisle,* p. 179.
[26]If, as some writers suggest, the Mystics had to obey the precepts of fasting, it was only in force, like Ramadan, between sunrise and sunset: at nightfall they made up for the damage. See Ovid, *Fastes,* IV, 535.
[27]These pitch-pots have been rediscovered in modern times. (*Revue Générale de l'Architecture* (Paris, 1868), p. 13).
[28]See Goblet d'Alviella, *Inde et Himalaya,* 2nd edn., p. 94.
[29]*Revue Générale de l'Architecture* (1868), p. 149.
[30]Παννυχίδες, Aristophanes, *Ranae,* 370. Νύκτες μυστικαί, Sopater Διαίρεσίς ζητήματων, ed. Walz, part VIII, p. 121.
[31]This well, which was rediscovered at the end of the nineteenth century, is formed of many-cornered stones; the opening is encompassed by concentric circles which undoubtedly depict the grouping of the choruses. (*Bull. de Correspondance Hellén.,* part XVII, 1893, p. 196).
[32]The first methodical excavations on the site of the telesterion were undertaken at the beginning of the nineteenth century by English architects at the expense of Dilettanti, the Florentine society. They were resumed in 1860 by Francois Lenormant who made his results known in his *Recherches Archéologiques à Eleusis* (Paris, 1862) and in the *Revue Générale d'Architecture* (1868 and 1870). The investigations were finally completed between 1882 and 1887 by the Greek Archeological Society of Athens. ('Εφήμερις ἀρχαιολογική, 1883-1888).
[33]See the excellent guide: *Eleusis ses Mystères, ses Ruines et son Musée,* by M. Demetrios Philios, director of excavations (Athens, 1896), p. 55 and following.
[34]Eusebius, Preparatio Evangelica, part III, 12, ed. Vigerus, p. 116.
[35]Tertullian, *Ad Nationes II,* 17, ed. Rigaltius, p. 57.
[36]*Phaedrus,* 250 C.
[37]*Daremberg et Saglio,* part II, p. 576.
[38]Aug. Mommsen also believes that the sacred wakes occupied three consecutive evenings. *Feste der Stadt Athen* (Leipzig, 1898), p. 245.
[39]Plutarch, *De Anima,* fragm. VI, 2.
[40]One of my former pupils, at present connected with the Archaeological Museum in Brussels, Mr Jean de Mol, wrote to tell me that, in the two years he spent at the Ecole d'Athènes, he had several opportunities of visiting Eleusis. The presence of large underground areas has been established in front of the telesterion, against the parapets, but their condition is too poor to furnish any information about their purpose. They are not supports which were later filled in because of sucessive enlargements of the telesterion as stairs have been found. Some of these cellar areas, which lie much lower than the temple, date from the time of Pericles; the vaulting is supported by square pillars. They are usually referred to as 'storerooms' for want of a more accurate description. But that is simply an assumption.
[41]The bas-relief, which represents this scene, was first described by Francois Lenormant (*Gazette des Beaux-Arts,* 1860, 1st series, part VI, p. 69). It was discovered in Eleusis around 1860. It is usually taken to represent Triptolemus, as he receives his instructions from Demeter and Cora before leaving for his world-trip. But not a single one of the details which usually typify representations of Triptolemus are to be found here. One could not find better grounds for regarding this as a portrayal of a candidate being received by both goddesses. The figure of the

youth is more likely to be that of a mortal than that of a great spirit; the attitude of the character points to a scene of reception rather than a farewell. Even if the article which Demeter appears to be holding is a grain of corn, as Lenormant suggests, displaying it forms part of the ritual of the highest degree, as will be seen further on.

[42]Fragment, *De Anima,* VI, 2.

[43]This is also the opinion of Philios, *op cit.* p. 66 and following.

[44]*Phaedrus,* 250 C.

[45]Homeri Carmina, *In Cererem,* line 480 and following.

[46]This seems to be the purpose of the episode described by Appolodorus: Tὸνἰ οφαυτην της Κόϱης ἐπικαλουμένης ἐπικϱούειν τὸ καλουμένον ἤχειον (Appolodore, *Fragm. Historicum Graecorum,* frag. 36, part I, p. 434).

[47]Homeri Carmina, *In Cererem,* lines 401-403.

[48]The details are described by Claudius. *De raptu Proserpinae,* lines 12-17. They can also be seen on various painted vases. See Overbeck, *Kunstmthologie, Atlas,* part IV, pl. 15 and 16.

[49]*Encyclopaedia Britannica,* under 'Mysteries'.

[50]Seneca, *Naturales Quaestiones* lib. VII, 31.

[51]*Vita Demetrii,* ch. 26 (Didot), p. 1075.

[52]It may be assumed however that Epoptism took place on the twenty-third, on the assumption that the ceremonies of the Great Mysteries, including the pilgrimage to the stations of Demeter, the visit to the Underworld and the Elysian Fields and finally the exhibition of the *hiera,* were spread over the two preceding evenings.

[53]Alb. Dumont, *De Plumbeis apud Graecos Tesseris* (Thorin, Paris, 1870), pp. 76-97 and *Bull. de corr. Hellèn* (1884), pl. 2, No. 42.

[54]The insertion of this episode, violently attacked by the Fathers of the Church, seems to be confirmed by the scholiast of Plato: 'Ετελειτο ταυτα και Δηοι και Κόϱη ὅτι ταυτην μὲν Πλούτων ἁϱπάξειε Δεοι δὲ μιγείη Ζευς, *Scholia in Gorgiam* (Bekker, Berlin, 1823), p. 354. According to some Church Fathers, Zeus had two marriages, the first with Demeter, the second with Cora, the daughter of this union. Out of this marriage, which Zeus contracted in the form of a snake, the monster with the bull's head was born (*Protrept. II,* pp. 13-15). But it is not definite that Clement of Alexandria did not purposely confuse the rites and the myths of different Mysteries.

[55]'Ιεϱὸν ἕτεκε ποτνια κουϱον βϱιμὼ βϱιμον, *Philosophumena,* V, I, 164 (Migne), p. 3149.

[56]Clement of Alexandria, *Protrept.* (Potter), pp. 14-19.

[57]The greatest, the most wonderful, the most perfect secret of Epoptism. *Philosoph. V,* (Migne), p. 3149.

[58]Brugsch, *Religion der alten Egypter,* p. 621.

[59]Overbeek, *Kunstmythologie, Atlas,* part IV, pl. 16, fig. 10 and *Daremberg et Saglio,* part II, fig. 2643.

[60]*Protreptique II,* publ. Petter, p. 14. The allusion to the pastos confirms the supposition that a representation of a sacred marriage was actually witnessed.

[61]Sir F. J. F. Marchal, 'Réponse à un passage des Recherches sur les Mystères des anciens, concennant le dogme de l'unité de Dieu, par le baron de Sainte-Croix' in *Bull. de l'Ac. Royale de Belgique,* 1851, part XVIII, part II, pp. 82-98.

[62]*Mathematica I,* p. 18; *Daremberg et Saglio,* part 2, p. 575.

[63]Theodoret, *De fide. ed. de Paris* (1642), part 4, p. 482.

[64]Harpocration, quoted by Lenormant in *Daremberg et Saglio,* part 2, p. 537, col. 2.

[65]*Corpus Inscript. Attic.,* part 2, No. 628.

[66]The formula reproduced imperfectly by Proclus and by the author of the *Philosophumena* is restored by an inscription found around the edge of a well near the Dipylon gate. The somewhat hasty conclusion was drawn that the rite was performed, not in Eleusis, but in Athens on the return of the initiates.

[67]*Hemenwap Southwestern Archaeological Expedition,* p. 3.

[68]*Religion of the Semites* (London, 1894), p. 231.

CHAPTER 2
THE ORIGIN OF THE GREAT MYSTERIES

The Greeks gave the name 'Mysteries' to certain rites exclusively known to those who were initiated. According to the information which has been handed down to us, these Mysteries had the following characteristics in common:

1. The fulfilment of preparatory or purifying formalities which brought the profane to a state of readiness to receive the initiation.
2. Transfer of 'sacred objects' (Παράδοσις των ἱερων). These ἱερά were sometimes formulas taught orally (Λεγόμενα, Συνθηματα) and sometimes symbolic objects which were put on exhibition or were handled by the neophyte (Δεικνύμενα, Δρώμενα).
3. Performance of mythological legends, either by priests or by the neophytes themselves.
4. The absolute prohibition of revealing to the profane the actions or words which formed the secrets (τὰ ἀπορρητα) of the intitation.[1]

I shall consider later if there is reason to add a fifth element to this summary: the communication of dogma concerning the life hereafter or mythology.

With respect to their origin, the Mysteries can be divided into two groups: those which originated in the early days of the Greek community, such as the Mysteries, which were celebrated in honour of the ancient native gods in Samothrace, Eleusis, Aegina, Argos, Arcadia and Crete; and those which are related to Eastern religions introduced at a later period, such as the Mysteries in honour of Dionysus the Phrygian, of Cybele and Attis, Adonis, Isis and finally Mithras. The most important and well known of them are the Eleusinian Mysteries.

One school of thought, the school of symbolic evidence, which flourished during the first half of the nineteenth century considered the Mysteries to be a priestly institution, intended, under the cloak of symbols borrowed from the customary polytheism, to preserve the philosophical naturalism which had originally characterized the religion. Dupuis, who attributes to them the aim of bettering the race, saw in them the work of 'legislators' who had taken it upon themselves 'to lead man through idle fancies to what is right.'[2] Less grandiloquently, Creuzer makes them a place of assembly for the philosophical dogma which 'the wise men from the East' had entrusted to Egyptian priests and which was conveyed by them to the Pelasgians of Greece.[3] Lobeck naturally reacted by asserting that they could be reduced to pure farce, or at least to the remnants of barbaric rites which were enveloped in darkness so as to conceal their crudity, at a time when people began to be ashamed of them.[4] The views of Lobeck, disputed by Guigniaut, Maury and Preller, have now been taken up again but with less prejudice by Andrew Lang who has soon made them accepted, thanks to his animated style and not least through is extensive ethnographical knowledge.[5]

But the conflict does not date from recent times. Philosophers of the Graeco-Roman era were overwhelming in their praise of the extent and influence of the Mysteries. 'It is said', relates Diodorus of Sicily, 'that those who have participated in the Mysteries are more devout, more honest and better in all respects.' Isocrates, Cicero, Plutarch and Porphyrus did not differ. On the other hand, the early defenders of Christianity, Clement of Alexandria, Tertullian, Eusebius, Gregory of Nazianza, Arnobe, etc. can find no mockery sharp enough, no accusations fierce enough against an institution which, in their eyes, united the immorality of the predictions with the ungodliness of the belief. Like Lobeck they believed that the Mysteries were celebrated in the dark because people were ashamed to bring them into the light of day. 'Nocturnal ceremonies', exclaimed Gregory of Nazianza, 'which deserve to be buried in silence.[6]

It would appear that, of the two attitudes, the former found its origin in the ideas which were associated with the Mysteries in the last period of the activity; the latter, in the remaining traces of the barbaric beginnings of the institution. Let us try to discover where the truth lies.

Magic Guilds

It would be a waste of time to discuss the starting point of the symbolic school. Like other religious institutions in ancient times, the Mysteries have their roots in an era when the peoples of Greece were very close to barbarism. Their early motives, therefore, would not have been higher than those found at the lowest rungs of civilization.

The existence of religious organizations which impose silence on their members is, among uncivilized people, an almost universal consequence of belief in the practice of witchcraft. Magicians who claim to have the power to command spirits seek followers everywhere—just as a workman seeks apprentices—and then impart to them by degrees the secrets of their profession.[7]

They sometimes find it advantageous to form a closed organization and thus we have the first form of a secret society, often under the protection of a special deity.

Among the North American Indians there exist societies of medicine men who come from different tribes, have complicated initiations and perform magic dances in different disguises.[8] Among the Kaffers, the 'rainmakers' have formed the society of the 'Intongas' which elects its followers from individuals who have a tendency to hysteria and visions.[9] In West Africa there are numerous organizations for fetish priests. There are secret societies whose members celebrate their rites deep in the forest, form noisy processions and make rich capital out of the fear of the profane.[10] In Gabon, one of these societies consists only of women who, painted red and white, go in procession to their sanctuary in the forest, playing tambourines and dancing wildly as in the Bacchanalia of former times.[11] In Polynesia, a society united magicians with priests. It was the guild of the Areoi, dedicated to the worship of the god Aro. They had seven degrees of initiation and the level of the members could be distinguished by special tatoos and ornaments. To be accepted into the order, one had to give proof of divine inspiration, ecstasy, etc. The novitiate was very strict; new tests were imposed to pass from one degree to the other. The initiates from the highest degree were treated as superhuman beings and after death went straight to the paradise of the Polynesians. The order organized plays depicting the legend of the god.[12]

It is easy to see that the purpose of these secret societies is the same everywhere: that of bringing the initiates into contact with superhuman power and communicating secrets which enable them to control their destiny. Even more singular is the fact that the same forms and similar methods have been adopted everywhere. Andrew Lang points out that the four following characteristics are found, not only in the Greek Mysteries, but also in those of Africa, America and Australia: (i) Magical dances; (ii) the use of the rattle (*crécelle,* bull-roarer, *turndun,* ῥόμβος); (iii) the custom of smearing the neophytes with clay or some other greasy substance which is afterwards carefully washed off; and (iv) exercises with tame snakes.[13] The clever folklorist could add further similarities: preparatory fasts; animal sacrifices; the use of disguises; and the temporary simulation of death, either by briefly burying the neophyte or by taking him on a journey through the realm of the dead.

Sacra Gentilicia

Does it then follow that the Greek Mysteries were exclusively collections of magical prescriptions, used for the personal interest of a few doctors in the art of magic? Even if we accept that they were at the beginning simple conjurations, real 'medicine dances', we can still wonder if their origin should not be sought in local ceremonies which imposed initiation formalities on foreigners. Lobeck himself gave a little thought to this possibility, when deriving certain Mysteries from the *sacradomestica,* in which a foreigner could not take part unless he has been specially admitted.[14] Ottfried Muller, for his part, sees a connection between the oldest Mysteries and Pelasgian religious ceremonies which were changed into secret rites when the Pelasgians were under the yoke of the Greeks.[15]

On the other hand, Robertson Smith has, in his profound studies into Semitic religions, attributed a similar origin to the Mysteries which are found among the Semites and especially among the mixed population in Asia Minor.[16]

As soon as conjuration ceremonies are no longer used for purely personal goals, perhaps in conflict with the interests of the tribe or town, but for the general benefit of the community, they assume a social character. The magic then ceases to be witchcraft and becomes religion.

When two neighbouring enthnographical communities go and live on the same land, either by conquest or by immigration, each of them initially retains its own gods and ceremonies as well as its customs and language. It is quite inevitable that a longing to win the ancient gods of the land for themselves evokes a desire in the new inhabitants to take part in some indigenous ceremonies. For this purpose they must be instructed by qualified initiators. Gradually these ceremonies cease to be the exclusive monopoly of a single race and as the mixing of the people increases, they endeavour, by winning followers, to replace birth by initiation.

At a time when Jahveh was exclusively the god of the Israelites, the Bible relates that settlers, who were brought by King Salmanazar from Chaldea to Samaria, had to endure wild animals because they did not know how to serve the god of the land: it is written that they approached the king of Assyria and requested that he should send them a priest of Jahveh who could teach them 'how they should fear the Lord'.[17]

The contrary is likewise true when it is the subjugated people who wish to be converted to the national religion of their conquerors. Amongst the Persians, Mazdaiism was a national religion: people were born as worshippers at the same time of Ormuzd, Mithras and as a Mede or Persian. When this religion was spread over Western Asia, following the conquering of the Archemenides, followers had to be obtained by initiation and in this way the Mysteries of Mithras came into being.[18] It can be seen that these Mysteries profited by changing a national or local religion into something which was universal.

The oldest Mysteries of Greece were, in that historic era, the inheritance of priest families which represented the remains of Pelasgian or Thracian tribes.

The Curetes, who were initiated into the mysteries of the Cretan Zeus, formed a hereditary society. Tradition had preserved the memory of a tribe of Pelasgians who bore their name and who seem to have lived on the northern bank of the Gulf of Corinth.[19] The Mysteries of Samothrace were passed off as an institution of the Kabires. Whether the name 'Kabires' is of Phoenician origin or not ('Kabirim' means 'the Great Ones')[20] is of no importance. These legendary children of Hephaestos and the daughter of Proteus could well be a personification of the early island inhabitants of the Thracian sea, who were skilled in both the working of metal and in the art of navigation. Pindarus connects them with the Curetes and the Korybantes after mentioning that the Kabires were among the people thought in certain Greek provinces to be the ancestors of mankind.[21] Perhaps they formed a tribe of smiths, like the Telchines; the art of forging metals must have been thought a secretive and superhuman ability in the eyes of those people who had hardly grown out of the Stone Age period.[22]

The Mysteries of Eleusis appear under the same circumstances. They were the inheritance of a group of families, connected with the Thracian immigrations, who ruled in Eleusis when this town was still free.[23] Their original purpose was to ensure the fertility of the fields belonging to the community. Only later was this purpose, which had the communal interests at heart, replaced by individual realization of the 'beautiful expectations' (Χαλαὶ ελπίδες), i.e. the attainment of salvation by the initiates after death. I believe that it is possible to reconstruct the principal phases of this process of evolution.

Farming Ceremonies of the Indo-Europeans

There was a time—before the historical era—when the farmers of Attica tried to ensure a successful harvest by naïve ceremonies, of which traces can be found in the folklore of all Indo-European people.

The important investigations of Mannhardt have clearly established that the Teutons, the Celts and the Slavs attributed to every field, or rather every piece of cultivated land, a spirit which personified the corn and the plants.

This spirit, whose existence is still believed in by some of the farming folk of present-day Europe, is sometimes represented in the form of a human being and sometimes as an animal. According to the region, this spirit may be called: the Mother, the Queen, the Old One, Granny. And again, if it is related to the harvest of the following year, it may be referred to as: the Daughter, the Maiden, the Child (Cornbaby), the Bride (May-Bride); or it may be given the name of Wolf, Dog, Hen, Sow, Mare, etc.[24]

In certain parts of Germany, when the wind bends the corn, the farmer cries out: 'There goes the Grain Mother'; in other provinces: 'The Wolf [or the Horse] is trotting through the fields'.[25] The Bogyman is used everywhere to prevent the children from walking through the corn. In Swabia, the one who reaps the last sheaf is said to 'have the sow'.

In Shropshire, the last sheaf is called the 'Mare'.[26] In the neighbourhood of Rijssel the reapers dance round the last sheaf shouting, 'There is the remainder of the Horse'.[27]

When the harvest has been brought in, its spirit remains in the last sheaf to pass from it to the new harvest. In Styria, the stalks of the last sheaf are made into a crown which is consecrated in Church the day before Easter; the grains of corn are then removed and scattered over the budding corn.[28] Amongst the Zapothecs in Mexico, the last bundle of maize was similarly placed on the altar of the local god and removed at sowing time to be buried in the middle of the fields, wrapped in an animal skin. If the harvest was abundant, it was dug up again and the grains were distributed among the families who kept them as a talisman for prosperity.[29] The Dajaks of Borneo, who are still in an age of spiritualism, clearly show us the original reason for these customs. At the time of harvest, their priest transfers the rice spirit into a handful of grains which are lying on an altar; these grains are then mixed with the seed for the following harvest.[30]

It is worth noting that this reasoning is simply a rendering in mythological language of the natural process which ensures the renewal of the harvest. The whole question lies in determining the manner in which the life in the corn is transferred. Where we think we see a propagation phenomenon, the imagination of early man saw a transfer of the soul, a rebirth.

The Rejuvenation of the Spirit of the Harvest

Just as our farmers are mindful of preventing spoilage of the grain, which carries the future harvest in its bud, so our distant forefathers endeavoured to prevent the spirit, which had to give life to the following harvest, from disappearing or degenerating while awaiting the sowing season. Now the spirit as well as the body is exposed to old age and decay. It was thus prudent to allow it to undergo a rejuvenation, to bring it to a rebirth. On the other hand, it had to be forced to enter its new body i.e. the next harvest. From both points of view it was necessary to destroy the former wrappings. The sheaf is therefore burned after its honour has been proven, and it is this ash which is mixed with the seed or scattered in the furrows.

In Bulgaria the last sheaf is still made into a doll which is dressed in women's clothes and called the Corn Queen; it is carried around the village, burnt and the ash is spread over the fields.[31] We have here the irresistible tendency again to give the fetish (i.e. the object which is considered to be inhabited by a spirit) the appearance which the people themselves attribute to the spirit.[32] Wherever we encounter the belief in the magical powers of the last sheaf, we see it embellished with womanly attributes: in Germany, Russia, France, Scandinavia and England, as well as in India and Middle America. We can also see almost everywhere that this doll is sacrificed so as to give the soul the opportunity of passing into a new harvest. In Silesia, the farmers fight over the charred remains, and if they do not bury them in their fields, they hang them up in the trees of their garden.[33] In Brittany, the last sheaf which is made into a doll and called the 'Mother-Sheaf' also includes a second image which is smaller and obviously represents the child in its mother's womb—Demeter, pregnant with Cora.[34]

It can also happen that the spirit of the last, still standing, sheaf passes into the body of an animal or even a person. The same treatment will now be applied or appear to be applied either to the reaper who made the last cut, to a stranger who happens to appear in the neighbourhood at that time, or to some creature, either tame or wild, which has been brought along for that purpose or has been found in the vicinity, especially if it is an animal of a kind which has lent its appearance to the spirit.

At the end of harvest around Grenoble, they used to sacrifice a goat which had first been allowed to walk over the farmland; part of it was roasted and later eaten, the rest was salted and kept until the next harvest.[35] In Tonilly, near Dijon, a cow was treated in the same way after being led over the fields.[36] In Transylvania the last sheaf is often called the 'Hen'; in Udharkély, a hen was tied to the sheaf and then killed with a spear; its feathers were mixed with the grain and scattered in the furrows at ploughing time.[37] In Saxen-Meiningen, the bones of the pigs which were killed at Christmas or Candlemas were kept until the sowing season and then buried in the field or put in the grain sacks.[38] When the barley is sown in Neuhaus, Kürland, the sower eats from a piece of back of pork, which still includes the tail, then buries the appendage in his field. It is claimed that the corn will grow to the length of that tail.[39]

If the spirit passes into the body of the woman reaper who reaped the last ears of corn, she receives the name of 'Mother', 'the Old One', 'Queen', 'Daughter', 'Bride', or 'Wife'. She is no longer put to death when sowing time comes round, but there are indications that there was a time when people pretended to kill the unfortunate stranger who had just been called to serve as a substitute for the spirit of the reaped harvest.[40] Sometimes the natural procedure of an imaginary procreation was simulated. In West Prussia, the Grain Mother, i.e. the woman reaper who was the last to finish her work, acts as though she is seized by the pain of giving birth. Some child or other is taken and declared to be her son; the boy is well wrapped up and carried in a bag to the barn.[41] In Scotland, where the young girl who has reaped the last sheaf bears the name of 'Queen', people are content to predict that she will marry within a year.[42]

The more or less openly recognized purpose of all these customs is to ensure a rich harvest. They date from a time when people were familiar with the notion of a community, but still imagined that the communal organism had its own soul and its own life and, like the personality of individuals, was subject to death and revival. They are connected, as Frazer has clearly demonstrated, with a religious situation where there are no priests, temples or gods, only spirits, each with its special domain in the revelations of nature, and where the rites have a more magical than conciliatory purport.[43]

Prototypes of Demeter

It is an indisputable fact that the ancestors of the Greeks passed through this psychological phase, common to all Indo-European people. Whether the name 'Demeter' is translated as the 'mother of the barley spelt'[44] (from the Cretan *δηαί* for *ξειαί*, barley or spelt) or, along with d'Arbois de Jubainville[45] as 'Foster-Mother' (from the root 'dhê' for 'thê'—from the Thracian 'dê' meaning 'to suck' or 'to suckle') or, according to the customary derivation, as the 'Earth-Mother' (Δῆ or Δα for Υη-μήτνϱ), this goddess is still to be found in the 'Korn-Mutter' of Teutonic people; just as the prototype of Cora survives in the 'Maiden' of the Scottish fields.

I do not know if there are any legends in modern folk-lore linking the daughter with the mother. But wherever a marriage between harvesters is simulated, the bride or bridegroom is often represented as having been lost and found again or having fallen asleep and awoken.[46] Even in the Pomeranian countries, the simulated birth of a child, which will represent the spirit of the next harvest, has its counterpart in the classical legend of Demeter who, through the embraces of Jaison, the Sower, becomes pregnant three times by Plontos, the spirit of abundance, in a furrow ploughed in the Rarian Field.[47]

At the beginning, therefore, there were as many Demeters as there were farmed estates. These local spirits were sometimes represented by a living animal or a woman, and sometimes by a sheaf or a doll more or less roughly adorned as a woman. Only the human form has continued to exist in honour of Demeter. But the image of this goddess remains continually linked with ears of corn and sheaves. The decoration on an Apulian vase shows us the worship of corn ears placed in a *naos,* without any representation of the goddess herself.[48] It is difficult to escape the conclusion that we are dealing here with an old survival of sculpture inspired by Demeter. The nickname of the goddess are all derived from the same line of thought: 'Ιουλω (the sheaf), 'Αξηοία (the dried grain of corn), Σιτώ (the grain), Χλοη (verdant).[49] The songs in her honour were called Ουλοι 'Ιουλοι and began with the cry 'Oulé! oulé!'[50]

On the other hand, in Phigalia, in Arcadia, Demeter is represented with the head and the mane of a mare.[51] Folk mythology tried to pass on this image in the rather scandalizing story of her relationship with Poseidon, by changing the goddess into a mare. It is very simple to explain this idea if we connect her with the European belief in the Harvest Horse or the Grain Mare. An oracle of the Pythia, reproduced by Pausanias, calls the sanctuary of Phigalia 'the cave which serves as a refuge for Deo the Mother of the Horse', (Ἱππολεχής).[52]

On the coins of Corcyra, Demeter was portrayed by a cow suckling a heifer. With reference to Demeter, Lenormant acknowledges, in the superb article written about Ceres for the *Dictionnaire Daremberg et Saglio,* that she can also be symbolized by the figure of a cow.[53] This symbol is most likely to be a vague memory. On terracotta vases the goddess is certainly portrayed with a heifer on her lap.[54] They did not dare show her suckling, as on certain Egyptian and Eastern representations of Goddess-Mothers;[55] but the intention was there, or at least had been. Every summer the cow was ceremoniously led to the sanctuary of Demeter by the inhabitants of Hermione, dressed in white and crowned with hyacinths. There it was sacrificed by old women with sickles, and it was undoubtedly, originally, a harvest cow, i.e. an antiquated form of Demeter herself.[56]

One may wonder if the same significance should not be attached to the snake, whose presence in the sanctuary of Demeter in Eleusis was drawn attention to by Hesiodus when he called it 'minister of the goddess' (ἀμφίπολος).[57] Sometimes the snake is drawing Demeter's chariot;[58] sometimes she has it on her lap where it is stroked by the Mystics.[59] Sometimes it curls itself around her sceptre or her torch.[60] In certain representations it even coils itself around her body.[61] Modern archaeology has now revealed that when certain animals appear as the regular companions of a god, or if they are sacrificed to him more than other kinds, these animals often represent the early form of the god himself. Although the comparison may be displeasing, the use of pigs is, however, founded on equally probable suppositions. The important role played by the sacrifice of the pig in the worship of Demeter, and particularly in the Mysteries, is already known. The goddess is sometimes portrayed with a pig in her arms.[62] A dissertation by Lucian, first published in 1870 by Mr Rolde, informs us that in Halimonte, on the occasion of the Thesmophoria, the women had the custom of sacrificing pigs to Demeter and Persephone; these were thrown with cakes and fir-tree branches into a cave inhabited by snakes. Sometime later, the women descended into the cave, chased away the snakes and retrieved the remains of the sacrifice. These pieces were laid on the altar and then mixed with the seed with the aim of ensuring a rich harvest.[63] The Greeks sometimes related that a herd of swine, grazing on the spot where Hades disappeared into the earth with Cora, was dragged down into the abyss with them. Sometimes it was said that these animals had hampered the search by Demeter by erasing the traces of the abduction.[64] We do not need these subtle explanations to recognize a survival from an era when Demeter was the Harvest Sow.[65] In bidding farewell to this Demetrian menagerie, I should like to add that the texts concerning the animals connected with the goddess also name the crane, the goat and the hen.[66] These animals complete the list of those which serve to incarnate the spirit of the harvest.

Amalgamation of the Corn Mothers

Whereas amongst other European people, the development of religion took place side by side and above folk tradition, Greek folklore gradually developed in the direction of the rich polytheism which already seems to have been fully formed in pre-Homeric times. When people saw that the harvest spirit was the same everywhere and that it did not need to be incarnated every year—in other words, that it governed the consecutive harvests from outside—the numerous Harvest Mothers, whatever their form, then amalgamated fairly easily. The amalgamation took place to the benefit of the local spirit called Demeter.

Not so long ago, during the harvest celebrations in the neighbourhood of Auxerre, the doll put on the bonfire to invoke a favourable harvest was called Ceres.[67] As Mannhardt notes, the use of this name merely signifies that the schoolmaster had had some say in the matter. But the process must have been the same in pre-Homeric Greece. Cretans must certainly have said to Ionians in Crete or Africa, 'We know your Corn Mother; it is our Demeter'. For the Cretans, Demeter was the 'Spelt Mother'. For the Greeks who spoke other dialects, 'Demeter' was a proper name, the name of the goddess who, from Olympus, fulfilled the functions of the former Corn Mothers.

According to Diodorus, the Cretans were sure that Demeter had gone from their island to Attica and from there to the whole of Greece.[68]

The Corn Daughters, the Coras, underwent the same treatment as the Mothers; they were also fused into one. Both goddesses should logically have become one, and later there was an attempt to do just that.[69] But at the time when the principal gods of the Greek pantheon acquired their definitive form, their individual identities were too strong for them to be unified.

Demeter remained the Foster Mother, *par excellence,* who made the harvest grow and mourned its periodical disappearance, just as a mother mourns over the abduction of her daughter. Cora, on the contrary, remained the spirit of the coming harvest, the personification of the seed which remained for part of the year under the ground. The tendency to compare gods with human beings, contributed to making Cora the wife of the god who ruled over the Underworld.

The Abduction and the Return of Cora

At this period, the marriage was made even more solemn by simulating an abduction. In Ancient Athens, married couples shared a cake, *πλακους γαμιχος*, made of flour and sesame.[70] According to a legend from Samos, Zeno ceremoniously celebrated his marriage to Hera in this way.[71] Denys van Halicarnassus even goes so far as to give this form of marriage the name of 'hierosgamos'.[72] Hades made Cora eat a pomegranate seed; although the goddess was abducted against her will, she would never be able to leave her abductor.

This is fundamentally the thought emphasized so clearly by Robertson Smith: sharing the same food means being imbued with the same nature and thus being bound to the same fate. It is interesting to follow the application of this principle, not only in the inviolability of marriage but also in what could be termed the association of man with the power of the dead. This is particularly so in those nations who have in their mythology the legend of a living man who temporarily descends into the abode of the dead. In the Finish heroic poem, Waenaemoïnen only returns to earth because he has refused to drink the beer of Tuonetar, the Queen of the Dead.[73] A similar adventure is recounted amongst the Sioux of North America, in which a hero returns from the Underworld because he has not touched a meal of rice on the advice of one of his uncles who descended before him into the abode of darkness. According to New Zealand tradition, a Maori girl, who has penetrated the realm of souls, receives similar advice from her dead father and thus refuses the food which is offered her.[74]

It is clear that the adventures of Demeter and Cora, as seen in Homer's Hymn, have been considerably developed. It is felt that Greek humanism applied itself to uniting and dramatizing them. In order to find out what they must have been like in their original simplicity, one must turn to the myths in which some peoples, still at the level of animism, have tried to clarify the origin of their rites by means of adventures which they ascribe to supernatural beings. Here, for example, follows a myth which a Belgian missionary, Father de Smet, noted around 1840 amongst the Potorvotomis of North America.[75] It is very interesting to compare it with the drama of Demeter.

The Manitos were jealous of both the brothers Nanabouzon and Chipiapous. When the latter had ventured alone on a frozen lake, he vanished in the water thanks to their witchcraft.

Nanabouzon declared war on the Manitos and travelled lamenting through the land, and after blackening his face, he remained sitting for six years without ceasing to speak the name Chipiapous.

The terrified Manitos then built a lodge where they invited the brother of their victim to a ceremonial meal. He accepted the invitation, and after washing his face, took a drink which was made from medicinal herbs. His sorrow immediately left him while those present abandoned themselves to magic songs and dances which were the origin of the great Medicine dance.

The Manitos brought Chipiapous back to life, but since he was forbidden to go into his brother's lodge, the latter gave him the rule over the kingdom of the dead.

Before he leaves, Nanabouzon initiates all members of his family into the secrets of the great dance and gives each of them a bag (with the talismans) with the order to pass it down to their descendants.

When Hades fell in love with Cora, he carried her off into the bowels of the earth when she once happened to go into the meadow alone without her mother.

Demeter travelled lamenting throughout the land, and then disguised as an old woman, sat down on a stone; she stayed at the court of the king of Eleusis where in deep sorrow she took neither food nor drink for nine days. Cora's mother, cheered up by a joke from the maid Iambe, finally drank some cyceon, a mixture of flour and water with mint, and after laying aside her disguise, she consented to take up her abode in the temple which had been built for her by the king of Eleusis. She proceeded to condemn nature to infertility, whilst she was far away from Olympus, so that the gods came to an arrangement to give her back her daughter.

It was agreed that Cora should return every spring to spend four months with her mother, but for the rest of the year she must share the throne of Hades in the Underworld.

Demeter returns to Olympus but first instructs Triptolemus to teach the knowledge of farming and Celeos to pass on the knowledge of the Mysteries to his descendants.

Since there is little likelihood that Father de Smet reproduced the mythology of the Iroquois under the influence of Greek poetry, we must accept that there was a spontaneous blooming in the native traditions of the New World of all the elements which, amongst such a gifted race as the Greeks, could give rise to the legend of the Homeric Hymn.

The Earth Goddess of the Pelasgians

The mythological assembly and adaptation which ended in the worship of Demeter, must have taken place during the centuries which followed the settling of the Thracians amongst the Pelasgian people of the Aegean Sea. I can find no well-founded reasons to doubt the traditional view that the Thracians were responsible for the introduction or at least the perfection of agriculture in Attica. We may similarly accept that the Thracians were the founders of Eleusis. But the Pelasgians had an Earth Goddess who could also lay a claim to the name of Harvest-Mother. 'It is the earth', sang the Peleades priestesses in Dodone, 'which brings forth the fruit; give the earth the name of Mother.'[76] So Demeter was made the Earth Mother. For a spouse she was sometimes given Zeus, who was connected with the Underworld and shown as the master and the distributor of the underground riches, and sometimes the god of water, Poseidon Pater, who encloses the earth in his moist embrace. The fusion is particularly obvious in the Demeter who was worshipped in Argos under the name of Pelasgis and in Hermione as Chtonia.[77]

Amongst the gods who had the right to the first fruits of the harvest, an Athenian decree from the fifth century B.C.[78] names, with Demeter and Cora, a couple who are only described as 'the god and goddess'. This anonymity makes one suspect that they are old Pelasgian gods, if one follows Herodotes in accepting that the Pelasgians had the custom of giving their gods neither name nor attribute.[79] But objects from a later period, found in the same regions, reveal the appearance of both these gods. One is represented by a bearded person on a bas-relief from the first century A.D., bearing the name Πλούτων.[80] This was, therefore, the Zeus of the Underworld. With respect to his anonymous companion, whom Foucart compares with Persephone, could she not have originally been the god Gé Kourothrophos who was worshipped in an Athenian Temple along with Demeter?[81] Pausanias states that Gé, Demeter and Cora were also worshipped together in Patrae in Archaia.[82]

Public Worship of Demeter

At the time of the Doric invasion, worship of both goddesses was certainly fully organized. Herodotus tells us that the Dorians tried in vain to banish it from the Peloponesus.[83] Even the worship of the Eleusinian Demeter seems to be older than the Ionic migration in the eleventh century B.C., because the Ionians took it with them to the colonies they established in Ephesus, Smyrna and Milet.[84]

It undoubtedly included festivals which resembled those celebrated in honour of Demeter more or less everywhere in Attica. An inscription discovered in Eleusis some years ago mentions among the festivals which were celebrated in honour of the goddess since time immemorial: the Chloia, when the corn sprouted out of the earth; the Kalamaia, when it began to ripen; and the Haloa when it was brought to the threshing floor. Perhaps we should add the sacrifices of the Proerosia fulfilled by the Athenians at the time of ploughing, and even the Thesmophoria, before this particular festival of sowing time was connected with the establishment of the family and ownership.

In its entirety, this cult involved sacrifices, national assemblies, exhibition of symbols, especially phallic emblems, and finally songs and games. It was, in short, a development from the ceremonies practised by the early farming communities of Attica and gradually connected with the higher idea, which was from then onwards built up from the supernatural powers. It was accepted that the gods were free to accept or refuse the sacrifices from their worshippers. From a pure act of magic, killing sacrificial animals became a sacrifice intended to make the gods favourably disposed. Some sacrifices could only be undertaken by priests or certain families. There were ceremonies exclusively intended for women. Nevertheless, within these limitations the worship of these great goddesses had nothing secretive about it.[85]

The Secret Ceremonies of the Eumolpides

What, then, did the Mysteries conceal? Alongside the rites, which were, so to speak, for the common good, there were in Eleusis, as elsewhere, other rites which the Eleusinians, or rather the members of certain families, had retained for their own secret use. When speaking about Athens, Alfred Maury writes: 'Although in some cities the tribes had amalgamated into one people and commonly worshipped their different gods together in communal ceremonies, some of them also retained their own secret form of worship.'[86] That was also the case with Eleusis, as testified by the allusions to the patrimonial traditions of the Eumolpides τὰ πάτρια των Εὐμολπιδων,[87] which are so frequently encountered in texts and inscriptions. These traditions not only formed the secret cult of the Eumolpides, but also of the Kerykes, the Croconides, the Coeronides, the Phytalides, etc.[88] One of these branches, the Hycomides, settled early on in Phlia, taking with them the ceremonies of Eleusis.[89] These families, of Thracian origin, all celebrated in the sowing or harvest season a religious festival that consisted of two different parts: (i) a foregoing initiation for children who had reached a certain age; perhaps for women who had entered the *génè* by marriage, and perhaps also for foreigners who were included. This initiation also included a journey through the realm of the dead; (ii) a number of ceremonies which were intended to exercise influence on the local harvest. These ceremonies included: a presentation of the adventures of the grain, personified by Cora; the exhibition of sacred objects, which possessed the value of a talisman; and, finally, various conjurations.

Many scholars believe the highlight of the ritual to be in the mystical drama. This belief is wrong, in so far as it sees the nucleus of the Mysteries in the revelation of the adventures of Demeter and her daughter. The theme of Eleusinian drama was never esoteric.[90] It is explained from beginning to end, not only in the Homeric Hymn to Demeter and in other poems—such as the now lost songs of Pamphos and Achilocus, which could possibly be called liturgical—but also in purely profane works, such as the essays or poems which Apollodorus, Ovid, Claudius and Nonnus dedicated to the same topic, without incurring the slightest reproach for indiscretion. Even the variations on the legend which undoubtedly had their origin in the local Eleusinian traditions—such as the events connected with Demeter's stay in this city—had long since been absorbed into the foundation of Greek mythology. It is probable, though, that the presentation of the abduction and the return of Cora was shown in itself as magic which could influence the abundance of the harvest, or rather the success of the sowing. This success depends, even today, on meteorological conditions which elude the actions and even the preventative measures of man. Farming is thus most suitable ground for superstition and folk-magic. How much more important the practices—which I have mentioned, following Mannhardt and Frazer—must have been in communities where they were contested by neither scholarship nor religion! While the ceremonies, which constituted the official cult, had become propitiatory actions, the ceremonies of the Mysteries retained the conjurational and, so to speak, mechanical power of an *opus operatum.* The divine majesty and autonomy, which in future would have to be taken into account, were sufficiently guaranteed by the assertion that Demeter herself had given the Eleusinian leaders these means to control the forces of nature directly.[91]

Precisely because they are founded on the general conclusions of sympathetic magic, the conjurations with an agricultural purpose in mind present a family resemblance which has led many to the wrong conclusion that this was a case of mutual borrowing. The festivals with which the Phoenicians celebrated the death or resurrection of Adonis—or rather his descent into the Underworld and his return to earth—were shown as indispensable ceremonies for obtaining fertility in the fields, herds and families.[92] Again and again, one comes across the notion that the transfer or awakening of life is furthered by its expression in a play. Amongst uncivilized people, this line of thought has often led to the same outcome, i.e. to essentially dramatic performances which show the changes which would be willingly observed in the natural course of events.

Walter Fewkes had described the partly public, partly secret, ceremonies performed by the guilds of the Antilope and the Snake among the Canadian Mogins to obtain rain.[93] We see priests, or rather magicians, performing sacrifices and fumigations, intoning ritual songs in honour of the spirits, executing mystical dances in which they use snakes and have ears of corn in their mouth, and finally, in an underground journey in the presence of the initiates, expressing by means of mime the adventures of a character called Ti-yo, his descent into the world of the spirits, the trials he undergoes and his return among the living whom he teaches the ceremonies for making rain. The highlight of the festivals, which last ten days, is the closing ceremony in which snakes are bathed or washed in a consecrated liquid after which they are released.

This last episode corresponds to the ceremony at the end of the Eleusinian Mysteries in which water from two pots is tipped over the earth while the Hierophant pronounces the clear, explanatory sentence, 'Be fertile, bring forth, bring forth to the utmost'.[94] In

Eleusis, in historic times, the only value of the ceremony was perhaps tradition. A writer, however, from the second century A.D. describes it as 'the great and secret Mystery of Eleusis'.[95]

The Admission of Foreigners

Charms of every category form secrets which people prefer to keep to themselves, and which it would be imprudent to confide to anyone else. The Eumolpides would, therefore, take great care in retaining the monopoly of the ceremonies for themselves and, for even greater security, would claim that Demeter had commanded it. On the other hand, the extraordinary fertility of their fields had to arouse the admiration and envy of their neighbours. The latter finally received initiation into the secret cult of the Eumolpides without needing to undergo the formalities of admission to the *génè*. At that moment the *sacra gentilicia* changed into Mysteries. Lobeck and Guigniaut have appreciated the distinction which their successors sometimes lost sight of. 'The *sacra gentilicia*', writes Guigniaut, 'were exclusive rather than secret; the Mysteries were secret rather than exclusive'.[96]

This change had several important consequences. There were, henceforth, two kinds of participants: the members of the Demeter *génè,* who held authority both with respect to the admission of the profane and to the organization of the Mysteries, and the ever-increasing number of foreigners who, once initiated, could attend the ceremonies and derive personal benefit from them.

This change perhaps took place as a consequence of the war between Eleusis and her close neighbour, Athens. There must be a grain of reality in this conflict which has been preserved in the legends of Attica. In it the descendants of Eumolpus lost their sovereignty but retained their cult;[97] and since the Athenians insisted on being admitted, the necessity for the initiation allowed the vanquished not only to retain their spiritual power but also to become the religious teachers first of the conquerors, then of the Hellenic world and finally of the Graeco-Roman community. The Mysteries of Eleusis can certainly be numbered among the religious institutions which had contributed the most to the development of the Greek sense of solidarity. When Callias, the Daduchus, was sent as envoy to the Lacedemonians to ask for peace, he revealed what services Athens had rendered to the other Greeks by offering the Mysteries. 'It is Triptolemus', he tells them, referring to the tradition of Athens, 'who was the first to open the sacred Mysteries to foreigners, particularly to the founder of your race, Hercules, and to your fellow countrymen, the Dioscuri.'[98] A few centuries later this national institution would become cosmopolitan and Aristides was then able to cry, 'Eleusis is the communal sanctuary for the whole world.'[99]

[1]One wonders how such a competent and judicious writer as Alfred Maury could assert that the Mysteries did not necessarily contain secrets. 'They were simply symbolic ceremonies,' he said, 'true priestly performances.' (*Histoire des religions de la Grèce antique,* (Paris, 1857), part II, p. 378). Acording to this criterion, the whole of pagan liturgy would consist of Mysteries! The Greeks themselves derived μυστήρια from μύω, meaning, 'to close (the mouth)'. In reality, the celebration of the Mysteries could contain some public ceremonies, but their principal element still remained a secret, with its necessary consequence: the initiation.

[2]Dupuis, *Origine de tous les cultes* (Paris, 1796), part II, 2nd part, p. 112 and following.

[3]*Religions de l'antiquité,* Acad. Guigniaut (Paris), part II, 2nd part, p. 752 and following.

[4]Lobeck, *Aglaophamus* (Koningsbergen, 1822), part I.

[5]Andrew Lang, *Myth, Ritual and Religion* (London, 1887), part I, ch. 9.

[6]Gregoire de Nazianza, *Sermo* (Paris, 1609), p. 625.

[7]Albert Réville, *Religions des peuples non-civilisés* (Paris, 1883), part I, pp. 294, 347, 378; part II, p. 177.

[8]Schoolcraft, *History of Indian Tribes* (New York, 1839), part IV, p. 430 and part V, p. 421. See the collection of publications of the Bureau of Ethnography, parts I to XVI, Washington 1891-1897.

[9]G. Frisch, *Die Eingeborenen Süd. Afrikas* (Breslau, 1872), p. 99.

[10]Wilson, *Western Africa* (London, 1856), p. 391 and following.

[11]*Ibid,* p. 393.

[12]W. Ellis, *Polynesian Researches* (London, 1853), part I, p. 229.

[13]A, Lang, *Ritual and Religion* (London, 1887), part I, p. 282.

[14]*Aglaophamus,* p. 270.

[15]Article 'Eleusinien' in the *Algemeine Encyclopädie,* sect. I, part XXXIII.

[16]Robertson Smith, *Religion of the Semites* (London, 1894), p. 358.

[17]2 Kings, 17: 25-29.

[18]F. Cumont, *Mystères de Mithra* (Brussels, 1899), part I, pp. 233-239.

[19]Homer makes the Curetes an earlier people from Etolia (*Iliad,* IX, 249). Strabo places them in Arcania (X, 3, 1).

[20]According to Salomon Reinach, the Pelasgian gods were 'the Great Gods' whose name the Phoenicians, who were in communication with Samothrace, absorbed into their own language (*Revue arch.,* part XXXI, 1893, p. 60).

[21]According to a passage in the *Philosophumena,* V, 1 (Paris, 1860), pp. 142-143.

[22]The smiths in the north-west of the Sudan still form a caste which is described as having magical powers (A. Revelli, *Religions of Uncivilized Peoples,* part I, p. 40).

[23]Traditionally Eumolpus, the name-giving forerunner of the Eumolpides, is considered a Thracian who is represented as the organizer of the Mysteries (Strabo,

VII, 7, 1; Pausanias, I, 38, 2). The myth writers make him sometimes a son of Poseidon and Chione (the snow) and at other times a son of Borus (the North Wind). (See Mauray, *Relig. de la Grèce antique,* part II, p. 217).

[24]Mannhardt, *Mythologische Forschungen* (Strasbourg, 1884), p. 296 and following.

[25]Mannhardt, *loc. cit.,* p. 167.

[26]Frazer, *The Golden Bough* (London, 1890), part II, pp. 24 and 27.

[27]Mannhardt, *Myth* (Forsch.), p. 167.

[28]*Ibid.,* p. 317.

[29]Brasseur de Bourbourg, *Histoire des nations civilisées du Mexique* (Paris, 1858), part III, p. 40.

[30]Spencer, St. John, *Life in the Forests of the Far East,* part I, p. 187 and following.

[31]Mannhardt, *Myth* (Forsch.), p. 332.

[32]See: Goblet d'Alviella, 'Les origines de l'idolâtrie' in the *Revue de l'Histoire des Religions* (Paris, 1885), part XII, p. 20.

[33]Mannhardt, *Myth* (Forsch.), p. 318.

[34]Sebillot, *Coutumes populaires, de la Haute-Bretagne* (Paris, 1886), p. 306.

[35]Frazer, *The Golden Bough,* part I, p. 15.

[36]Mannhardt, *Myth* (Forsch.), p. 60.

[37]Mannhardt, *Die Kornämonen* (Berlin, 1868), p. 15.

[38]*Id, Myth* (Forsch.), p. 187.

[39]*Ibid.,* p. 186.

[40]*Ibid.,* pp. 39-40, 47.

[41]*Id, Die Korndämonen,* p. 28.

[42]Frazer, *The Golden Bough,* part I, p. 345.

[43]*Ibid.,* p. 348 and following.

[44]*Myth* (Forsch.), p. 292 and following.

[45]*Les premiers habitants de l'Europe,* 2nd edn. (1899), p. 290.

[46]The awakening of the Sleeping Beauty in the forest by her future husband has its counterpart in certain parts of Russia and France where, on May 1st, a young girl, the May Bride, wakes a young man who is pretending to sleep under a pile of twigs or flowers (Mannhardt, *Korndämonen,* p. 341, 344).

[47]*Odyssée,* V, 125 and following.

[48]*Gazette archéologique* (1879), p. 32.

[49]Lenormant in, *Daremberg and Saglio,* part I, 2nd edn., p. 1036.

[50]Maury, *Rel. de la Grèce antique,* part II, p. 133.

[51]Pausanias, VIII 42, 3.

[52]Pausanias, VIII, 42, 6. There was a statue of a horse in the Eleusinion in Athens. (Id, I, 14, 3).

[53]*Dictionnaire des Antiquités,* part I, 2nd edn., p. 1067.

[54]Claraa, *Monuments de Sculpture,* pl. 438. E, no. 786 F.

[55]Ledrain, *Gazette archéologique* (1877), p. 135. Also, Lonpérier, *Athenaeum francais* (1855), p. 24.

[56]Pausanias II, 35, 3-7. Pausanias adds that in the secret part of the temple, there stood a secret image which only the old sacrificial priestesses understood. This image was undoubtedly, as in Phigalia, the theriomorphic portrayal of the deity.

[57]Strabo, lib. IX, ch. 1.

[58]Overbeck, *Kunstmythologie,* Atlas, pl. 17, No. 24.

[59]*Ibid.,* pl. 16, No. 1b.
[60]*Archaeol. Zeitung* (1852), pl. 38.
[61]Overbeck, *Atlas,* pl. 16, No. 8. Also, Millingen, *Ancient Conis,* pl. 5, No. 8.
[62]In the Louvre there is a small terracotta statue showing the goddess holding a torch in one hand and a piglet in the other.
[63]Frazer, *Pausanias,* part V, p. 29.
[64]*Id, Pausanias,* p. I, 14, 3.
[65]Singular irony of history! The scholars from classical antiquity took great pains not to see that Demeter was sometimes a sow, and it was in a pig sty 'inter pullos et porcos' that Matthai in Moscow in 1780, discovered the text of the Homeric Hymn in which the legend of the goddess assumed its most human and poetic form. (Letter from Ruhnken reproduced in Hignard, *Des Hymnes Homériques* (Paris, 1864), p. 292).
[66]The hen was also dedicated to Persephone. On an object illustrated in the *Annales de l'Institut d'Archéologie* of Rome, the goddess sitting next to Hades, holds a hen in one hand and a bundle of corn ears in the other. (1847, part XIX, pl. F).
[67]Mannhardt, *Myth* (Forsch.), p. 319.
[68]Diodorus, V, 77. I note here that in the Homeric Hymn to Demeter, the latter, on revealing herself to the daughters of Celeos, says that she comes from Crete. (*In Cererem,* line 123).
[69]Both goddesses often appear on the same objects; they are given the same characteristics and the same appellations; they sometimes share the same throne. 'Both', writes the scholiast of Euripides, 'are called Demeter, the younger as well as the elder.' (*Ad. Phoeniss.,* 689).
[70]Iwan Muller, *Handbuch des klassischen Altertums Wissenschaft* (Nordlingen, 1887), part IV, p. 147, c.
[71]Athénée, *Deipnosophistae,* lib. XV, 672b (Leipzig, 1868), part IV, p. 112.
[72]*Roman, Antiquit.,* II, 25, 4-5 (Didot), p. 87.
[73]Léouson-Leduc, *Le Kalevala,* 16th Runo (Paris, 1868), p. 139.
[74]Edw. B. Tylor, *Civilisation primitive* (Paris, 1868), part II, pp. 68-69. Tylor adds: 'There may be a similarity between these legends and the episode in Homer concerning the lotus-eaters.'
[75]De Smet, *Mission de l'Orégon* (Gand, 1848), part I, p. 284, and following. M. A. Lang has also quoted this legend as an example of similarity with the legends of the Greek Mysteries (*Myth, Ritual and Religion,* part II, p. 270).
[76]Pausanias X, 12, 10.
[77]The sanctuary of Argos was said to stem from Pelasgos, son of Triopas, and that of Argos, from a collateral branch of the Pelasgians, the Dryopes. (Pausanias II, 2-4, and 35, 3.).
[78]*Bulletin de correspondance hellénique,* A. IV (1880), p. 227, No. 35.
[79]Noted by Toutain, (*Revue de l'histoire des religions,* part XLV, p. 400).
[80]Foucart, *Recherches sur les Mystères d'Eleusis.* 1st account, p. 26.
[81]Pausanias I, 22, 3.
[82]Pausanias VII, 21, 4.
[83]Herodotus II, 117.
[84]Ottfried Muller established this fact for Ephesus, basing his opinion on a passage from Strabo which relates that in this city the Nelides or Androlides, as well as the King-Archon of Athens had retained the title βασιλευς and the privilege of

sacrificing to Demeter. (Article 'Eleusinia' in the *Algemeine Encyclopädie,* sect. I, part XXXIII, p. 274). Foucart reaches the same conclusion for Milet by connecting the existence of a month Kalamaion in the Milesian calendar, with the festival of Kalamaia. (*Revue des études grecques,* 1893, p. 322).

[85]Foucart believes that the Haloa included a true initiation for women, led by the priestess of Demeter. (*Revue des études grecques,* 1893, p. 322). It is not certain that this initiation was connected with the Mysteries, although the priestess played a leading role in the latter, particularly in the presentation of the Mystical Drama.

[86]A. Maury, *Religions de la Grèce antique,* part II, p. 2.

[87]Cicero asked Atticus to send him an inscription of it from Athens.

[88]Foucart gives a full summary of this. (*Recherches sur les Mystères d'Eleusis,* 2nd account, Paris 1895, p. 20 and following).

[89]*Ibid.,* pp. 47-48.

[90]Homer calls the couple Persephone and Hades (*Iliad* IX, 456 and 569; *Odyssey* X, 491).

[91]Homeris Carmina, *In Cererem,* lines 473-478.

[92]C. P. Tiele, *Hist. des anciennes religions de l'Egypt et des peuples sémitiques* (Paris, 1882), p. 292.

[93]The snake dance of the Mogins of Arizona, in the fourth part of *Journal of American Ethnology and Archaeology* (Boston, 1894).

[94]ὕϵ, κύϵ, υπϵϱκύϵ, See above. In Holstein, one of the Central European countries where the farmer would rather close the heavenly sluices than open them, they still sprinkle water on the statue representing the Corn Mother after carrying it ceremoniously on the last cart. (Mannhardt, *Myth,* Forsch., p. 316).

[95]Τὸ *μέγα και ἄϱϱητον* 'Ελϵυσίνιων *μυστηϱυον*. *Philosophumena,* part V, 1.

[96]*Memoires de l'Institut de France* (Paris, 1857), part XXI, p. 40.

[97]Pausanias I, 38, 3.

[98]Xenophon, *Hellenica* VI, 3 (Didot), p. 447.

[99]Aristides, *Eleusinios* (Dindorf), p. 415. For a long time, foreigners who wanted to be admitted to the initiation had to become naturalized in Athens or be adopted by a citizen. But this custom fell into disuse. See Lenormant in, *Daremberg and Saglio,* part II, p. 556.

CHAPTER 3
THE ESCHATOLOGY OF THE MYSTERIES

In the last chapter I have tried to reconstruct the nucleus of the Mysteries. I have shown that, initially, there are grounds for differentiating between the actual initiation and the secret ceremonies which were the principal purpose of the institution.[1] The purpose was to obtain a successful harvest for the families devoted to the worship of the Eleusinian goddesses, Τὰ γένη τὰ περὶ τὼ Θεώ, and in a wider sense, to ensure that the initiates prospered. Now when the Homeric Hymn was written to Demeter, at the end of the eighth or beginning of the seventh century B.C. we can see that the Mysteries had a quite different purpose: to ensure their followers' happiness in the life hereafter. How did this change come about?

Initiation Among Uncivilized People

If we wish to reconstruct the antecedents of an institution which reaches back to prehistoric times in Greece, we should do well to consult once again corresponding customs which, among uncivilized people, seem to be the result of a process of reasoning which all humanity has in common in the early stages of their spiritual development.

In Australia, amongst the natives of New South Wales, boys who have reached the age of puberty, are abducted by a character called Thuremlin, who seemingly kills them, cuts them in pieces and then calls them back to life.[2] Along the river Darling, this initiation includes the following ceremony. The neophytes are taken to a grave in which, under a thin layer of soil, lies an old man, holding a branch in his hand. As a magical song is chanted, he begins to wave the branch about and finally rises up.[3] Could one not read here the description given by Firmicus Maternus of the 'passion' of Dionysus, when he shows the god stretched out in the darkness on his bed of state, 'His death was mourned with bitter laments, then a light was brought and the Hierophant poured water over the neophyte and then slowly sang the following distich, 'Courage, Mystics; now your god is saved, salvation also awaits you!'[4] In Polynesia, on the Fiji islands, the young boys are led before a row of men who are lying down representing corpses, covered with pigs' blood. On a cry from the priest, they suddenly arise, and while the ceremony continues, they go and wash themselves in the nearby river.[5]

In some parts of the Congo, the young men who have reached the age of manhood fall down as though dead. They are taken by the magicians to the forest where they stay for several months, even years, after which they return to their family but must behave as though they have forgotten everything from their former life, even the language and the habit of feeding themselves. They have to be fed again as though they are new-born babies.[6] Similar singularities are encountered among the Virginian Red Indians and the natives of New Guinea. Among the latter, the neophytes are forced into the mouth of a monster which resembles a cassowary or a crocodile; it is then said that the devil has swallowed them and, while the mothers lament, the neophytes are led blindfold into a dark cave where the magicians, making an infernal noise, pretend to knock off their heads. After eight or nine days, they are taught the customs of the society and the tribal traditions; they are ordered to keep silent about what they have seen and heard and are finally returned to their families. But here too they must act as though their whole education has to be repeated, as though they were small children.[7] According to Frazer, the purpose of these ceremonies is either to protect the soul of the young men temporarily against certain dangers or to give them a new soul borrowed from some kind of totem.[8] The second explanation sounds by far the most probable to me, on condition that we do not limit ourselves to the sphere of totemism but also look for the subject, which the initiates must become familiar with. The subject may lie among the spirits of the plants, the waters, the heavenly bodies, or some mythical ancestor or a powerful magician; in other words amongst all who possess superhuman power.

Initiation = Regeneration

In order to obtain a new soul, the old one must be relinquished, that is to say, one has to die first. Therefore most initiations include an apparent death; the neophyte may be subjected to a simulated sacrifice or a journey through the land of the dead may be imposed on him. 'To die', said Plutarch, with a play on words, 'is to be initiated' (*τελευτᾶν* = *τελεισθαί*).[9] One could add, vice versa, that initiation is to die. It is at least a temporary death in order to return to life under other and better conditions. From this aspect, initiation is really regeneration. This is the way it was regarded by the Ancients and uncivilized people whose customs I have already described.

We can see from the tale of Apulaeus that initiation into the Mysteries of Isis was shown as a voluntary death which led to another life. The Mysteries of Cybele included the sacrifice of a ram and a bull whereby the candidate, lying in a grave, was sprinkled with the blood of either animal. From that moment on, he was 'taurobolio criobolique in aeternum renatus'.[10] Nowadays, in India, a young Brahmin who wishes to be initiated into the knowledge of the Veda by a guru must submit to a ceremony which takes him back to a so-called embryonic state.[11] Finally Christian baptism, which is the principal formality for admission to the community of believers, is always represented as a symbolic funeral with the goal of a spiritual resurrection.[12] On the architrave of the baptistry in Latran, the oldest in contemporary Christendom, one can read the following maxim which Pope Sixtus III had engraved on it in the fifth century:

> Caelorum regnum sperate, hoc fonte renati;
> Non recipit felix vita semel genitos.

In certain religious orders, the ceremony of taking vows, which is a true initiation, includes a funeral service which is held for the novitiate who lies in a coffin or under a shroud between four candles. After the Miserere has been sung he stands up, goes to each person present and, receiving the kiss of peace, is then given communion by the abbot.[13] From that day onwards, he assumes a new name which he will keep until his death.

The Initiation of Children in Eleusis

There are indications that originally in Greece young boys sometimes had to undergo very severe initiation tests, such as the whipping of young men on the altar of Artemius Orthia in Sparta[14] and on the grave of Pelops in Olympia.[15] Perhaps the ritual child sacrifices, which local legends speak of and which have been compared to similar sacrifices among the Semites, are only a corruption of the initiation enactments in which they pretended to kill young men and subsequently give them a new life.

In the Mysteries of Eleusis, the inhabitants of Attica not only had the prerogative from childhood onwards to be admitted to the initiation on the suggestion of their father, but there were also certain children selected by fate from pure Athenian ancestry, who took part in the Great Mysteries with a special function. They were called „Παιδες ἀφ᾽ ἑστιας; μυηθέντες ἀφ᾽ ἑστιας", 'children' or 'initiates of the hearth'. They particularly carried out certain ceremonies of conciliation for the other candidates.[16] Guigniaut is of the opinion that in this way it was hoped to make a general penance more gratifying to the gods by allowing it to be performed by innocent hands! Alfred Maury limits himself to explaining the expression 'children of the hearth' by the fact that they stood closer to the sacrificial flame.[17]

Can we not see here a survival from the time when the children of the families who were in joint possession of the Eleusinian Mysteries were initiated by means of a kind of baptism or rebirth by fire? The desire to clarify this ceremony when its original significance had been wiped out, would certainly have brought about a myth such as that of Demaphon who links the Homeric Hymn to Demeter with the adventures of the goddess at the court of the Eleusinian king. Queen Metanire had entrusted her child to Deo, whose divine nature she was still unaware of. The goddess who wished to make her foster-child immortal, rubbed him with ambrosia and concealed him at night in a glowing hearth. Metanire, who surprised her when she was performing this last action, uttered a cry of shock and indignantly forced the goddess to abandon her plan. Demaphon remained, therefore, subject to death.[18]

A different interpretation, stated by Hygin, confirms the assumption that this concerns a myth which was formed in order to clarify an initiation ceremony; that it was the Eleusinian king who, through his impetuous interference, had broken the spell and that the goddess punished him by death;[19] the punishment still given to those who interrupt an initiation or betray the secret.

As far as I know, August Mommsen is the only writer who has felt a connection to exist between the myth of Demaphon and 'the children of the hearth', when he suggests that the latter light their torches from the sacred fire as a reminder of the immortality which the goddess had wished to ensure for Demaphon.[20]

I am of the opinion that this is a case where one is inclined to clarify the myth by the custom, rather than the custom by the myth.[21]

The 'passage through the elements', to use an expression of Apulaeus in the description of his initiation into the Mysteries of Isis,[22] is frequently shown in Antiquity as the condition necessary for the renewal of man. At a time when it was thought that the universe was composed of three or four simple elements, might not consideration of the physical phenomena which take place in the decomposition of living organisms lead to the conclusion that death gives back to their different reservoirs the water, air, fire and earth which unite to form the personality of man?[23] And it is precisely in the ceremonies of the Mysteries, with its implications of purification and renewal, that we find submersion or anointing, the use of the fan, the mediation of fire in the double form of fumigation and illumination and the descent into the Underworld. In any case, the latter formality, which was kept until the end of the Mysteries and took the form of a walk through Hades and the Elysian Fields, had the implications, for those who took part, of death followed by rebirth in better conditions than in the former life. It was a true rebirth through which everyone who wished to take part in the *sacra* of Eleusis for the first time had to pass. I have already shown how these *sacra* finally amalgamated with the preceding initiation. The rebirth of the profane was no longer an introduction but the principal part and eventually the principal aim of admission to the Mysteries; it was no longer represented as a fact of momentary Significance, but as a symbol and guarantee of the fate which awaited the initiate after death.

Life After Death in Homeric Times

The early Greeks, like all Indo-Europeans, believed in the presence in living beings of an element which was not the body but resembled it; it formed the true personality and after death lived on quite free from the body. This 'double' remained, wandering around in the vicinity of the body and, following the decomposition of the body, near the place of death. It could, in fact, move further afield so as to interfere in human affairs. The living could not get rid of it, only provide it with a suitable place of abode into which they compelled it to retreat by means of certain ceremonies and where they ensured it remained by providing for its post-earthly needs. The relatives had to fulfil this double mission but the whole community had a vested interest. Indeed, when the deceased was decently treated, he could exercise a very great influence on the living by means which are not clearly defined; he proceeded to protect his descendants and even his fellow-citizens—hence the reverence for heroes. If, on the contrary, no funeral services were held for him, the deceased was a public danger.

The necessities of the life hereafter were limited to accommodation and food. The graves were made in imitation of houses and either from fear, sense of duty or love, every man put into the tomb, according to his means, whatever might help the life of the inhabitants or render it more agreeable. Feasts were held at home in which the dead were supposed to participate; sacrificial offerings were killed on their tomb which sometimes had an opening in the wall through which the blood could reach the remains of the dead. The latter custom perhaps indicates an era in which some kind of obscure, continued existence in the body was accepted. However this may be, cremation, which destroyed the body, left nothing more than the shadow—the pale, almost effaced, but still redoubtable, image of the one who no longer lived.[24]

Imagination gradually fused the underground abodes of these countless 'doubles' into one. On the other side, or preferably, under the tomb, just as among the Semites—and perhaps due to the penetration of Semitic traditions, since this conception does not appear to exist among Eastern Arians—there was an opening to a kind of gigantic cave, the domain of Hades, where the souls whose ashes were left behind in their tombs, led a life which was a vague imitation of their earthly existence. This belief was dominant in Homeric times. The *Odyssey,* which in this respect is closer to

Egyptian tradition, places the entrance to Hades in the western region on the far side of the ocean stream where the sun disappeared every evening in the darkness.

In the twenty-forth song, the poet describes to us the departure of the shades. With his golden staff, Hermes herds together the souls of the Pretenders, killed by Ulysses, and shows them the way, 'whilst they toil behind him sighing like a flock of bats in a cave'. The god leads them 'to the other side of the ocean stream, past the White Rock, near the gates of the Sun, through the land of dreams, as far as the meadow of daffodils, the abode of spirits, where the shades of exhausted people live.'[25]

It is a gloomy, dank land, where only marsh-plants and drooping shrubs grow. The dead roam around in troops, weak, hungry, with neither will nor memory, without any motives other than a vague instinct which drives them there to seek the libations and the victims' blood which is shed for them.

In the eleventh song, when Ulysses has been through the land of the Cimmerians and approaches the entrance to the Underworld in the hope of questioning Tiresias' shade, he begins by digging a hole, then pours out wine, honey and water, sprinkled with a little flour, and finally the blood of a black sheep. The shades hasten at once to this offering and he has to fend them off with his sword so that they do not reach it before the person for whom he is waiting.

In the same place we find the very moving episode concerning his meeting with his mother who only recognizes him after drinking the black blood in her turn. He tries three times in vain to embrace the beloved shade; he grasps only air.[26] In another frequently quoted part, Achilles, who has tried in vain to grasp the shade of Patrocles, gives the following definition of what part of man continues to exist, 'Verily in the abode of Hades, there remains a soul and an image (*Ψυχή καὶ εἴδωγον*) but absolutely no content (*φϱενες*).'[27]

Everyone in this world of delusions retains his rank and even his pursuits; Minos continues to have the right to speak, Orion to hunt; these seem to be purely subjective mementoes which cannot make up for the loss of the earthly reality, and one can appreciate the melancholy of Achilles who would rather 'work the land for a master without family, estates or possessions, then rule over all those who have lived'.[28] Even for the rich and powerful, immortality was a bitter irony under these circumstances.

Early on, human imagination, which never loses its sense of

justice, asked itself the following question: does there not exist for certain privileged people any means of withdrawing from the disaster of a fate equal to destruction? At that time there were vague tales circulating about a distant land, the Islands of the Blessed, in the land of the setting sun, where beings which were neither gods nor men led a peaceful, endless existence in radiant bliss, in a constant climate. There reigned Kronos and the blond Rhadamante; Hesiodus was later to place the men of the fourth race there, the heroes of the wars of Thebes and Troy.[29] But in Homer, the only person actually to gain admittance is Menelaus because he was the son-in-law of Zeus through his marriage to Helena.[30]

The Elysian Fields naturally have their counterpart in an abode worse than Hades, Tartarus, where the pitiful existence of the majority of the dead is replaced by cruel torture, intended for the enemies of the gods, the infamous criminals who have infringed the divine law in particularly grievous circumstances: the Titans, Tantalus, Pirithous, Sisyphus, Ixion etc. But ordinary people were not fated to be a Titan, less still a Rhadamante or a Menelaus.

Change in the Purpose of the Mysteries

But meanwhile in the eighth century, a ray of hope falls on this gloomy conception which shocks the old idea of Hades to its very foundations. It arises from the Eleusinian Mysteries which henceforth offer their initiates the means of escaping from the quagmire of Hades. 'Happy is he', says the Homeric Hymn to Demeter, 'who has seen these sacred ceremonies. He who is not initiated and has not taken part in them, will not have the same fate after death in the cold regions of darkness.'[31] This is also echoed by Pindarus, Sophocles, Plato and Plutarch, although their conception of the life hereafter goes far beyond the materialistic conceptions in which the Hellenic imagination pictured itself at the start of blissfulness on the other side of the grave.

This change of purpose was considerably facilitated—but not caused, as was long thought—by the nature of the legends which formed the mythical history of both goddesses—Demeter, who took into her womb both the dead and the seed and could therefore provide them with a similar fate and Cora, the personification of this very seed, who descends into the Underworld every autumn, only to emerge every new season as young and fresh as ever.

In this way the grain of corn became the symbol of human

existence. In Attica, corn was sown on the tombs. According to Cicero, 'this took place so that the earth, cleansed by this seed, could be given back to the living.'[32] A modern hygienist would not express himself otherwise, although with a more realistic significance. Can one not see the real reasons for this custom amongst the Egyptians, in the identification of Osiris, or of the 'Osirisized' death, with a grain of corn or barley which opens out in the womb of the earth under the fertilizing influence of water? Amongst the paintings which adorn the roof of the great temple in Philae is a mummy lying in a sarcophagus from which parallel ears of corn are rising, watered by a priest. The inscription reads, according to Brugsch, 'This is the form of the unmentionable, secret Osiris who is speeding upwards.'[33] The closing ceremony of Epoptism, i.e. passing the ear of corn, harvested in silence, which the Hierophant showed to the neophytes as 'the' word of the Mysteries, was undoubtedly simply a farming ceremony; nothing needed to be changed to make it a symbol of human rebirth.

Even if this symbol can actually provide a representation or encourage an expectation, it still cannot be the source of the central concept and we should ask ourselves why the sight of mystic drama, or even the journey through the Underworld should ensure the bliss of life after death. It has been asserted that, by participating in the adventures and the suffering of the great goddesses, the Mystics also received the right to share their later fate. Others have quite simply assumed that the initiate received so many indulgences which he could use to advantage in the kingdom of the dead, or that once admitted to the fellowship of immortals, he could never fall back into the circumstances of ordinary souls. But nowhere in these suppositions can one see the logical connection between the result and the means.

If necessary we could content ourselves by accepting here also the principle of imitation magic which claims to create things by representing them. But I prefer the explanation put forward by Foucart.[34] I find it impossible to follow the view of the learned Hellenist that the Eleusinian Mysteries were originally Egyptian and that, initially at least, Isis and Demeter were equivalent. The Greeks, without doubt, borrowed a certain number of myths and even gods from various neighbours. But we have seen that the great goddesses have European origins. On the other hand, although such an old and direct influence as Egypt in the formation of the

Hellenistic pantheon is disputable, one may certainly assume with Foucart that the Greeks of the eighth or even the ninth century B.C. were fully aware of the Egyptian conceptions of the life to come, as a result of the percolation of ideas which did not supercede their own conceptions but rather defined or completed them.[35]

A Practical Course in the Geography of Hell

The Egyptians believed that geographical knowledge of the Underworld was essential for the deceased so as to enable him to reach the fields of Ialou where he would lead a peaceful, happy life. So they placed in the tomb a more or less complete example of the *Book of the Dead* which showed the road they should follow in the region on the other side, with the spells to be used against the spirits of Hell—a kind of Baedeker, or, to avoid using such an anachronism, a Pausanias of the other world, enriched with a vocabulary list for daily use. A similar lesson was given in the Mysteries where the neophytes were taken, full of anticipation, along the great road through the Underworld and Elysium. According to Foucart, the Hierophant revealed to the candidates, as the plays unfolded, the secrets entrusted to their forefather Eumolpus by the goddesses: the region of the Underworld, which they saw; the road to be followed; the true names of the friendly or hostile gods; the words which would have to be spoken in this or that place, etc.[36] This is the description given by Aristophanes, Plato and Plutarch, as far as they dared without running the risk of being accused of profanation.

Homer had already described in detail the principal lines of the geography of Hell. Paintings on vases show Hades as a gloomy place intersected by quagmires, meagre fields and shrivelled groves. In *The Frogs* by Aristophanes, Hercules, who visited the land on his search for Cerberus, shows the way to Dionysus who also wishes to risk the adventure: first a wide, deep bog, then a region 'ravaged by snakes and all kinds of terrible monsters; on one side a muddy abyss where the criminals have sunk; on the other side myrtle bushes, where groups of men and women in a clear light are cheering the beautiful concert of flutes'. 'Who are the blessed?', asks Dionysus. 'The initiated', replies Hercules. 'With regard to the road further on, the initiated will give the son of Semele all the direction he requires because they live right next to the Palace of Hades and on the road which leads there.'[37]

In support of his conclusions, Foucart refers to the golden plates which were found in the tombs of Petilia on Sicily and Eleutherna on Crete; as in the *Book of the Dead,* fragments have been found bearing journey descriptions and spells, to be used by the deceased.[38] These spells often betray an Orphean influence, but they are from a rather late date and there is nothing to prove that they are connected with dead people initiated into the Mysteries of Eleusis. No less ingenious is the comparison made by the same author between the name of the Eumolpides (those who sing well, from ευμελπω) and the little 'Ma Khroou', which the dead receive on Egyptian epitaphs. He notes that this name is translated by 'pure of voice'; he points out that the dead man is able to utter, with the inevitable intonations, the incantations which he must use against dangers in the other world.[39] The Eumolpides were those who had to pronounce and teach in precisely the right tone the formulas which were intended as passwords in the Kingdom of Hades. This purity of intonation was no less essential than the exact reproduction of the text. It was therefore particularly expected that the Hierophant should have a pure voice[40] and that the candidate should, *at the very least,* be reasonably articulate. It is at least this last statement which Foucart shows to have been in the exclusion formula spoken by the Hierophant against all who were φωνην ἀξύνετος.[41] Maspero has supported this theory with his high egyptological authority. In a review of Foucart's study, published in 1895 in the *Revue de l'Egypte,* he writes, 'Like the Hierophant in Eleusis, the Egyptian priest had to have a pure choice to begin the intonation of the formulas, and the candidate who was repeating after him likewise had to have a pure voice. Like the candidate in Eleusis, the Egyptian deceased followed his road past dangerous or beneficial springs and monsters which he drove away with his singing; he passed through intense darkness and arose on fertile islands, radiant with light, where Osiris offered him a peaceful retreat on condition that he knew the passwords.'

There is no doubt that the requirement for a 'pure voice' found acceptance in both the Egyptian Ritual of the Dead and the Greek Eleusinian liturgy; indeed, it belongs to the essential conditions for the success of the incantations—or these are connected with the vicissitudes of the future life or the use of supernatural power in general—and it appears in almost all ancient cults, from Chaldea and India to Egypt and Greece. On the other hand, Eumolpus was a singer and a poet, which explains his name quite naturally without the aid of an Egyptian translation. But the question becomes thornier if it comes to clarifying the resemblance in the application and even the content of the magical formulas.

The direct influence of Egypt on Greek civilization is hardly noticeable before the settlement of Ionic and Milesian colonies in the Delta under Psamnitik I (second half of the seventh century). Official connections between the two countries began even later when in 548 B.C. Ahmas sent a contribution to the Delphians for the rebuilding of the temple of Apollo which was destroyed by fire.[42] But one can ask oneself to what extent an indirect influence could have permeated many centuries earlier, if not through reputed Egyptian settlements, the existence of which in Greece remains somewhat doubtful, then through the civilization of the Mediterranean or preferably the Aegean Sea region which flourished around 2000 B.C. Through his major excavations at Knossos, Arthur Evans was able to establish that from the eighteenth dynasty, if not earlier, an exchange of industrial products and even religious symbols took place between the empire of Thebes and the legendary kingdom of Minos.[47] Excavations in Eleusis in the Acropolis have brought to light earthernware, sacrificial plates and even statues which are connected with this Aegean civilization, and in 1898 Foucart informed the Institut de France about a city of the dead in the same neighbourhood, where, in the fourth layer of graves, scarabs with hieroglyphic script and a statuette of Isis had been found.[44]

Nothing actually gives us the right to establish that Egypt passed on anything to Greece in this manner other than purely technical processes and some art motifs. I should personally prefer to support the Phoenician influences; Victor Bérard has revealed how important the Phoenician influence was on Greek mythology.[45] These model brokers, the Phoenicians, were not content to take *objets d'art,* which were usually decorated with religious subjects, from the Egyptian coast to all countries along the Mediterranean Sea; they were also able to furnish their clients with explanations which they had themselves learned concerning the significance of this decoration.

That was not enough to make the Greeks accept the Egyptian gods. But it is sufficient to certify that at a time before the seventh century B.C. they were influenced in their concepts of Tartarus and the Elysian Fields by the sculpture-descriptions of the Amenti and the fields of Ialou. This also indicates that, at a time when the Mysteries of Eleusis were still somewhat flexible, they introduced the Egyptian idea of providing their initiates with practical means so as to be able to make a successful journey through Hades.

Penetration of the Moral Conception

One can well understand that this attractive result would increase the influx to the Mysteries throughout the entire Greek world. For the very first time life's end was rid of its terrors. Man had conquered Hades: entry to the Elysian Fields was no longer the right of heroes alone; everyone who was initiated into the secrets of the great goddesses could share in it. Before long portraits of Demeter and Cora appeared on the sepulchral columns and sarcophagi as the guarantors and administrators of bliss in the other world. 'Thanks to the beautiful Mysteries, which we received from the gods', runs an inscription from a later date, 'death is no disaster for mortals, but rather a benefit'.[46]

Until this moment, there was, in the future life promised by the Mysteries, no mention of any moral reward. The initiation, and this alone—and under all circumstances—would ensure happiness in the other world. We can still find here the notion of *opus operatum,* combined, if Foucart's theory is correct, with a kind of geographical gnosticism.

In the meantime, moral consciousness, which had extended its field of activity, increasingly penetrated religion. The conception of a moral order, in accordance with the plan of the cosmic order, and likewise placed under divine protection, had gradually induced the Greeks to make their gods defenders of justice and to seek divine approval for the actions of man. In the sixth century B.C., the too frequently occurring contrast between unhappy virtue and triumphant sin caused the heart-rending doubt which comes to light in the hymns of Theognis: 'how canst thou, O son of Kronos, treat the untrustworthy and the righteous alike?'[47] There was certainly the traditional solution: 'Innocent children and the following generations pay the debts of their forefathers.' But the poet himself rebels against this transferability which places the responsibility for the debts on the heads of the innocent: 'Great Jupiter, if it pleases the gods that the villain enjoys crime, why does it then not please them that he should pay for the harm he has done without the father's transgressions being the cause of subsequent unhappiness to the children?'[48]

The philosophers then began to look in the possibilities of the life to come for a more just means to compensate for the irregularities of the present life. Pythagoras took refuge in the removal of the soul which he combined with the current traditions concerning Hades. According to his school of thought, Tartarus is a region of penance for souls who have lived badly and who, after undergoing their punishment, will return to assume a new body until they are sufficiently purified to be taken into the arms of God. Pindarus who reproduced in his odes the principal eschatological theories of his time, puts forward, among other things, the hypothesis that man passes over from the land of the living to that of the dead and vice versa, so that he is treated according to his merits in each of these consecutive lives: 'Those who during a three-fold stay in each of these regions have been able to keep their souls free from all injustice, follow the road of Zeus to the Islands of the Blessed.'[49]

Plato also accepts the mythological description of the other world, but he separates the dead according to their moral behaviour: the good in the Elysian Fields, the bad in Tartarus and those who were somewhere in between went to Hades or the bog of Acherusiades.[50]

This appearance of moral rewards in the destiny of the dead was a direct contradiction with the theory that happiness in the other world depended exclusively on participation in the ceremonies, and, long before Diogenes, the enlightened spirits must have faced with rising fear the problem which the philosophers of Sinope formulated as follows: 'Shall the robber Paetacio, because he is initiated, be happier after his death than Epaminondas who has not received initiation?'[51]

The concept of ritual purity was the breach penetrated by ethical thought in the Mystery-explanation. There was a time—in Greece as elsewhere—when 'unclean' was not yet dissociated from 'sacred', i.e. where the notion of blemish was confused with violation of 'taboos'. This last expression, which has been adopted in the history of religion and in ethnology, indicates both the social and religious regulations which forbid certain contacts and actions, either because they infringed the area of ever redoubtable, secretive powers, or simply because they had the result of causing the intervention of supernatural beings, considered to be damaging.[52]

Human blood—whether voluntarily or accidentally shed—is held, above all, to be a channel for noxious influences. Whoever comes into contact with it is exposed to the greatest dangers, but because he can pass this 'association' on to his blood relatives and even to all the members of his tribe, they are quick to isolate him; he is struck by a real anathema, which usually amounts to denying him water and fire.[53]

In Homeric times that was the fate of murderers and at a much later time, in Athens, they still put the inanimate objects which has caused the death of a citizen into real exile. Of what use is magic if it cannot more or less neutralize the effect of 'taboos'? It is thus accepted that in some cases purification processes can deliver the guilty or rather the imprudent from their compromising association with angry spirits. That is a perfectly consistent line of thought, traces of which are found in the origin of criminal law amongst the Greeks and the Semites as well as the Kaffers and the Polynesians.[54]

They gradually sought the source of the defilement incurred by the murderer less in the actual contact with blood than in the attack on the natural course of life, established by the gods who were the only masters of human life. From that moment on, the aim of purification was no longer so much to withdraw the guilty from the influence of the avenging Furies and give him back his full communal life, as to reconcile him with the higher gods. Even Apollo had to submit to purification in the valley of Tempe when he had killed the snake Python before he could take his place again among the immortals. Also, according to Eleusinian tradition, the Small Mysteries were established by Demeter to permit Hercules to be purified following the murder of the Centaurs.[55] Some crimes, however, were of too serious a nature for cleansing to be possible by the usual means of purification, for example, the killing of a fellow citizen or a guest, sacrilege, violating an oath, treason against the fatherland.[56] Thus, as a result of the advantages of the Mysteries, i.e. salvation in the life to come, certain people were excluded from initiation, not only those who were proved beyond doubt to have committed these misdeeds, but also those who were simply accused of them, as long as they had not justified themselves. In this way, the initiation was—or at least should have been—proof of good moral conduct, the privilege of innocence and, at least negatively, of virtue. But what was to happen to those who had participated in the Mysteries and, following their initiation, had committed some crime; or even those who, not withstanding the official ban, were able to penetrate the intimacy of the good goddesses with a stained conscience?

This is where Orphism intervenes, when it penetrates the Mysteries of Eleusis in pursuance of the worship of Dionysus.

[1]Could one not see an allusion to this distinction instead of a purely poetical superfluity in line 481 of the Homeric Hymn to Demeter where the poet successively calls the initiation and the participation in the Mysteries, Ος δ' ἀτελὴς ὑέρων, ὃς τ' ἄμμορος. Plato also uses two terms to describe the profane: ,,ἀμύητος καὶ ἀτελεστος'', unless this is only an allusion to the difference between Small and Great Mysteries. Likewise Andocides tells his judges, 'Thou art initiated and thou hast witnessed the ceremonies of both goddesses.' *Orat. Graec.* (Didot), part I, p. 53.

[2]A. L. P. Cameron, 'Tribes of New South Wales', in the *Journal of the Anthropological Institute* (London, 1885), part XIV, p. 358.

[3]A. Howitt, 'Australian Ceremonies of Initiation', in the *Journal of the Anthr. Inst.* (London, 1883-1884), part XIII, p. 453.

[4]Julius Firmicus Maternus, *De error, prof. relig.* (Rigaltius), p. 15.

[5]L. Fison, 'The Nanga', *Journal of the Anthr. Inst.* (London, 1884-1885), part XIII, p. 22.

[6]W. H. Bentley, *Life on the Congo* (London, 1887), p. 78 and following.

[7]Frazer, *The Golden Bough,* part I, p. 347 and following.

[8]*Ibid.,* part II, p. 54.

[9]*Ex Opere de Anima,* II, 5.

[10]*Corp. Insc. Lat.,* part VI, p. 97, No. 510.

[11]Satapatha Brahmana, 'Kanda II', *Sacred Books of the East,* part XLIV, pp. 86.90.

[12]Letter to the Romans, 6:4; Colossians, 2:12.

[13]See the ceremonial Benedictinum, according to the *Dictionnaire de theologie catholique* (Gaume, Paris, 1863), part XIX, pp. 184-185.

[14]Pausanias III, 16, 7.

[15]Maury, *Relig. de la Gr. Ant.,* II, p. 105.

[16]*Relig. de la Gr. Ant.,* II, p. 353.

[17]*Ibid.*

[18]Hom. Carmina, *In Cerer.,* line 232 and following.

[19]*Fabulae,* fab., 147 (Schmidt, Jena, 1872), p. 21.

[20]A. Mommsen, *Feste der Stadt Athen,* p. 274.

[21]In his work *The Jonah Legend: A Suggested Interpretation,* William Simpson develops with powerful arguments the view that the adventure of the Hebrew prophet is an interpretation of an initiation scene in which the neophyte has to remain three days, either dressed in fish-skin or representing a sea-monster in a performance of the Scheol.

[22]'Per omnia vectus elementa remeavi.' (Apuleus, *Metam. Lib.* XI, Didot).

[23]This idea is clearly expressed by Europides (*Frag. Euripid.,* Dubner, frag. 833).

[24]For belief in a continued existence during the pre-Homeric era, see Fustel de

Coulange, *La cité antique,* II, and E. Rohde, *Psyche* (Fribourg 1898).
[25]Song XXIV, line 1 and following.
[26]*Odyssey* XI line 108 and following.
[27]*Iliad* XXIII, 103-104.
[28]*Odyssey* XI, 597-600.
[29]*Opera et Dies,* lines 167-173.
[30]*Odyssey* IV, 561-569.
[31]*In Cerer.,* line 480 and following.
[32]Cicero, *De Legibus* II, 25.
[33]Brugsch, *Religion und Mythologie der alten Aegypter,* p. 621. M. J. Capart translates, 'It is the mystery of the unknown created by the new water.'
[34]*Recherches,* 1st review, 2nd part.
[35]If one wishes to find the foreign antecedents for the myth of Cora's abduction, could one not turn to Mesopotamia? Istar, who has descended into the Underworld to seek the one she loves is taken prisoner by the mistress of gloomy Arali. Her absence also makes the earth infertile so that the gods find it necessary to send a messenger to the Queen of the Underworld with the order to set her prisoner free. (See Sayce, *Religion of Ancient Babylonians,* London, 1879, p. 221 and following).
[36]Foucart, *Recherches,* 1st review, p. 63.
[37]*Ranae,* line 137 and following. In the tragedy *Heracles furieux,* Hercules adds when describing his journey to the Underworld: 'I succeeded because I have seen the sacred Mysteries.' (line 613).
[38]One of the inscriptions reads as follows: 'In the abode of Hades thou shalt find on the left a spring and next to it a white cypress. Take care not to approach this spring. Thou shalt find another from which flows fresh water which comes from the Lake of Memory; guards stand before it. Say to them: I am the child of the earth and the starry sky, but my origin is divine; which thou shouldst also know. I am dying of a consuming thirst; but give me without delay the fresh water which flows from the Lake of Memory. And they will give thee water from the divine spring and thou shalt reign henceforth among the heroes.' (Foucart, 1st review, p. 67).
[39]Maspero: *Etudes de Mythologie et d'Archéologie Egyptiennes,* part II, p. 373.
[40]Epictetus, *Dissert,* III, 21, p. 439 and following, Leipzig, 1749.
[41]Foucart, 1st review, p. 32 and following.
[42]Herodotes II, 180.
[43]Arthur J. Evans, 'The Palace of Knossos, in the *Annual of the School at Athens,* VI, (1899-1900). Also, *The Mycenaean Tree and Pillar Cult* (London, 1901), p. 48 and following.
[44]*Comptes rendus de l'Académie des Inscriptions et Belles Lettres.* Sitting of October 28th, 1898.
[45]Victor Berard, *Les Phéniciens et l'Odyssée* (Paris, 1902), part I.
[46]'Εφημερις 'Αρχαιολογικη, a journal of the archaeological society of Athens, 1883, p. 82.
[47]Theognis, *Eleg.,* line 377 and following.
[48]Line 731 and following.
[49]Pindarus, *Olump.* II, line 68 and following.
[50]*Phaedo,* LX-LXII.
[51]Plutarch, *De Audientispoetis. Moral.* (Didot), p. 26. See Diogenes, *Haertes,* VI, 2 (Didot), p. 142.

[52]See Leon Marillier, *Sur le caractère religieux du tabou mélanésien,* in part 4 published by the Section des Science Religieuses in the *Bibliothèque de l'Ecole des Hautes Etudes* (Paris, 1896), p. 35 and following.

[53]In *Oedipus Rex,* Oedipus cries out, after consulting the oracle about the plague which Thebes is suffering after the murder of Laios, 'Whoever this man may be, I order no one in this kingdom to receive him, speak to him, allow him to take part in prayers or sacrifices to the gods, give him entry to purification; all must exile him from their hearth, for he is the blemish which will defile us all as the oracle of Python has revealed to me.' *Oedipus Rex,* line 236 etc.

[54]With regard to the Semites, this point is excellently illustrated by Robertson Smith (*Religion of the Semites,* 11th lecture).

[55]Strabo IV, 14, 3.

[56]The chorus of Mystics in *The Frogs* clearly reproduces the precepts of the Mysteries when it tells the spectators, 'Far from here the bad citizen who stirs up the hearth of revolt in his own interest; who allows himself to be corrupted when the Fatherland is in danger and who hands over the fortresses and ships; the tax official who smuggles in forbidden food; he who provides the enemy fleet with money, who besmirches the images of Hecate by composing dithyrambs, who cuts the fee of the poets at the Dionysian celebrations.' *The Frogs,* line 354 and following.

CHAPTER 4
THE MYSTERIES AND ORPHISM

The Homeric Hymn to Demeter does not make any mention of Dionysus among the Eleusinian gods. We may suppose that this god gained admittance to Eleusis when the Small Mysteries, or Mysteries of Agra, which are also omitted from this hymn, were organized. According to Etienne de Byzance, the Mysteries of Agra celebrated the adventures of Dionysus. It is possible that they had first formed an independent centre in Athens; the Eumolpides must have annexed them as the first degree of initiation, so as to rid themselves of an annoying competitor. Tradition has it that they were originally established to extend the blessings of the initiation to foreigners.[1] However this may be, I am inclined to link the division into the Great and Small Mysteries to the changes undergone by the cults in Attica under the influence of the Cretan reformer Epimenides. I realize that all religious reforms are explained in this way when the ancestry is not found in the Athens of Solon. But one can justifiably emphasize that the rite of the Small Mysteries—as far as we know—consisted mainly of purification ceremonies.[2] It was precisely with the aim of organizing new purification ceremonies during the plague which followed the murder of Cylon, that the Athenians invoked the assistance of the

Cretan sage. Pausanias tells us that the statue of Epimenides stood before the Eleusinion in Athens. It has indeed been asserted that this statue could be connected with another person of the same name.[3] But the text of Pausanias definitely states that it refers to Epimenides of Knossos.[4]

The Mystical Development of the Cult of Dionysus

Even if the Athenian Dionysus at the beginning of the sixth century B.C. is not yet the great god of the Orphic festivals, he is no longer the simple spirit of the wine who led the wine-harvest in Homeric times. The oldest traditions show him traversing the woods and fields of Attica, Thrace and Boetia with a tumultuous following of nymphs and satyrs. 'The traditional festival of Dionysus', writes Plutarch, 'was formerly a simple, popular merry-making. At the head of the procession, a jar of wine and a vine tendril; then a goat, followed by a basket of figs and finally the phallus.'[5] Illustrations on vases show us representations of this rustic cult. The population of various villages attended this celebration to display the legendary thiasus of the god and from these naïve bacchanalia where many jokes were exchanged, ancient comedy appears to have developed. The Lenaea or feast of the winepress and the Anthesteria or flower-festival, which were celebrated in Athens in honour of Dionysus, are merely the development of this truly Flemish fair, removed to the sunny climate of Hellas. However, the Anthesteria already shows a tendency to make the wine spirit into the god of universal prosperity:[6] this naturally brought him closer to the two goddesses who were the personification of the fertility of nature.

Towards the end of the seventh century B.C., the influence of Asiatic religions began to spread; these nearly all portrayed a god who died in order to rise up again: Attis; Adonis; Sabazios; the sungod of the Phrygians; Zagreus; the 'Great Hunter' of Crete, etc. According to Herodotus, in around 600 B.C. Clisthenes, the tyrant of Sicyone, 'returned' to Dionysus the Lamenting Corn with which the suffering of the hero Adrastus was celebrated.[7] As Maury, following Ottfried Muller, has noted, Adrastus has some connection with Adonis and Attis; at the same time he appears to have been an altered form of Zagreus.[8] The cult of Zagreus seems to have spread in Greece even earlier: a line from *Alcmeonides* calls Zagreus 'the highest of all gods'.[9]

Meanwhile Dionysus can merely die to be resurrected. Is the grape not plucked, crushed in the press to be translated into a noble liquid? Dionysus is referred to, according to Plutarch, 'as a god who is lost, vanishes, leaves life, only to be re-awoken.'[10]

So they began to celebrate the suffering of Dionysus with alternate mourning and festivity. This only accentuated the orgiastic tendency of the cult. The formation then took place on Greek soil of Dionysian Mysteries with their Asiatic splendour and boisterous exaltation—the round dance of Bacchantes with hair hanging loose, the lewd, bloodthirsty rites which would penetrate as far as Rome.

The explanation of these ceremonies is found in the identification of Dionysus with vegetation principles of life. The wild screams and savage dances of the Bacchantes have the aim of waking the spirits of nature which have been sleeping throughout the winter. The blood of the victims, torn apart by the Maenads, takes us back to the time when it was believed that blood libations could stimulate the slumbering spirits to further activity. The spirits are represented by the satyrs who follow the god and frequently adopt an ithyphallic attitude as though to personify the powers of generation still further. Dionysus is called 'Ελευθεϱιος, the liberator (of the sleeping germs); Ψυσιξψος, the reviver; Πολυμοϱφος, he who assumes the most forms. The oldest representations of the god have been borrowed from the vegetable kingdom, recalled by the name 'Dendrites'. Among his attributes are found: the phallus; the horn of plenty; the thyrsus which he uses to make springs of water and wine flow. Flowers and fruit can be seen everywhere, springing up underfoot. His principal festivities are celebrated between the winter solstice and the spring equinox. In Delphi, Apollo replaced him, so to speak, during the winter months. 'At the beginning of winter', writes Plutarch, 'the dithyramb awakens, the paean is silent and for three months one god follows the other in the invocations.'[12]

It could not be more clearly shown that the cheerful Dionysus, the Apollo of winter, night (Νυκτελιος) or the Underworld (Χθόνιος), is a kind of Greek Osiris.[13] He has therefore become a double of Hades in his capacity as Πολυδεκτης, he who receives the multitude and as Πλουτοδότος, he who distributes the riches. He is even shown as the husband of Cora or even of Demeter. Thus the penetration of Eleusis has been prepared in a quite natural way, bringing concepts and ceremonies which, as Jules Girard has noted so well, will, on the one hand, bring the cult of the great goddesses a more passionate and more tragic accent, and on the other hand will define or develop the divine wisdom of the Mysteries according to Orphic dogma.

Orphism: A Method rather than a Doctrine

It is very difficult to give a coherent survey of what is known as Orphism. The name of this school covers a whole series of songs, poems and fragments which run from the sixth century B.C. to the last days of paganism. These works, which are neither signed nor dated by the true authors, mirror the ideas of all philosophical systems which followed each other from Pythagoras to the Neo-Platonists.[14] In reality, Orphism was—and this probably explains its success as well as its long life—more of a method than a doctrine; less an attempt to establish a new philosophy or even a religion, than an endeavour to bring mythical tradition into line with the requirements of the surrounding civilization, and to use the resources of religious feeling to the benefit of the philosophical schools in vogue. The only condition it placed on the systems to which it gave the help of its mysticism was that they should yield to the pantheistic tendency which had characterized the attempt by Greek thought to bring unity and harmony into the concept of the universe.

This tendency, which clearly comes to the fore in Plato and reaches its peak in Alexandrian philosophy, but which has been gradually developing since Thales and Pythagoras, actually ends by formulating a double concept: (i) 'behind any manifestation of nature is an indefinite Being which, for want of a better name, will be called Chaos, the Night, the Boundless Ocean or Boundless Time, the One, the Inexhaustible or the Unknown Father; (ii) from this indefinite and unknown Being proceeds a secret representative who works according to fixed rules and to whom in the last instance all phenomena of the universe may be traced. Some call it Zeus or Eros, others Nous or Pneuma, still others, Persephone or Nature; Plato creates it from the prototype (ἰδέα) of the universe; Philo calls it the Logos; Herbert Spencer, the Power or the Energy.[15]

It would take me too far from my subject if I were to investigate what part Eastern considerations could have played in the origin of this double concept. The originality of Greek thought lies particularly in its attempts to solve this problem which is all too often overlooked or superficially treated by West-Asia. How can one reconcile the destiny of cosmic development with the freedom and responsibility of man? In this field Orphism was both the consequence and the cause; it was influenced by the principal philosophical schools which were originally independent of it, and it again was influenced by the concept of the gods and the life hereafter which passed from religious contemplation to the field of philosophy. However difficult it is to classify the few documents which have reached us, we do have some starting points. We can include in the first period—which is of particular interest to us here—the fragments which are reproduced by writers from the period of Pericles. One can also grant a certain amount of credibility to the quotations provided for us by the writers of the following centuries and even from the last era if these passages are connected with writers whose works were then known and accessible. Finally, one should attribute to the latter periods of pagansim those poems which reproduce the concepts of Neo-Platonism such as the *Argonautica* and the *Lithica,* and also a collection of songs, prayers and litanies, intended for the purification ceremonies or the Mysteries. The latter documents are of particular value in that they furnish us with a terminal point in the theological development of the Mysteries.

Orphic Cosmogonies

Before the appearance of Orphism, Pherecydes and Pythagoras had already outlined unitarian systems of world genesis in which the great deities of mythology played a rôle. Onomacrites, who is said to have written the first Orphic books, attributed to Orpheus, Musaeus, Linos or other singers, lived in Athens under the Pisistratides, at the end of the sixth century B.C.[16] He was, perhaps, a disciple of the Pythagoreans, although he may have been their rival. He learned, if one may believe Sextus, Empiricus and Ausones, that fire, water and earth were the elements of the universe.[17] Through this he was connected with the precepts of the first natural philosophers of the Ionian school, only this school personified the elements under the name of the old gods;[18] and by applying the system of god-genesis, popularized by Hesiodus, Orphism made these gods of the elements descend through a whole line of generations from a first pair;[19] which was itself soon shown to be a division of one single Being. This Being (the First Substance, *οὐδία*, of the Pythagoreans) was called by the professors of Orphism, 'Chaos' or 'Night', i.e. infinite space, or 'Chronos', unlimited time.

It is impossible for us to establish which of these doctrines concerning the descent of the gods is the oldest in Orphism. The one which is connected with the personification of Chaos, seems simpler and fits better in the chain of mythology according to Hesiodus. The one which puts time at the beginning of things suggests a more abstract idea; it lies closer to Persian theory which puts Zervan Akarana, infinite time, above Ormuzd and Ahriman.[20]

In the first system, the followers of Orphism made Aither develop from Chaos, or the spiritual principle of each differentiation which, after thickening around the edges, with the help of Chaos, formed the Cosmic Egg.[21] In the second, the Cosmic Egg is likewise formed by Chaos and Aither, but Aither and Chaos both issue from Chronos which, according to Proclus, the followers of Orphism called 'the unpronounceable principle of all things'.[22] Both systems brought a wonderful being into existence from the Cosmic Egg, the personification of Light, Life and Understanding, the principle of Order and Harmony. This Being, 'begotten by secret lineage[23] sings of Orphism under the abstract names of 'Phanes' (he who differentiates), 'Metis' (the Meditation); or under the mythological forms of Eros, Zeus, Demeter, Persephone, Hades or Dionysus.[24] Their dogma on this point could have been formed before Plato, who describes as an old tradition (*παλαιὸς λόγος*) the notion that in God is the beginning, the end and the middle of all things.[25]

Once this idea of unity of the Supreme Spirit or the Universal Life was formed, the name by which it was called made very little difference. All the gods were equal beings, or at least mutually exchangeable, and could, turn by turn, take on the role of the uppermost god in the songs in which they were invoked. This is the religious state of affairs which Max Muller stamped with the name of 'haemotheism', including syncretism and symbolism which begins to increasingly characterize the divine dogma of ancient paganism. The Orphic Poems proclaim explicitly that Dionysus is none other than Zeus, Hades or Helios.[26] It is in fact always of nature (*Ψύσις*) or rather the life-force of the universe, that the poet sings:

> O, Nature, Queen-Mother of all things, inexhaustible mother, venerable, creative, she who tames all, unmentionable, brilliant, the first-born who annihilates all, who brings light . . . end, that takes no end; all communal, but not to share, born of yourself, present in everything and knowing everything . . . bitter for the wicked, kind to the holy—Blessed One, who makes things grow and decompose—father and mother of all things . . . universal worker, proceeding in an endless whirlpool, preserver, maintaining yourself through perpetual metamorphoses . . . Life everlasting, immortal Providence to whom everything belongs and who makes all things alone, I beg you to give me peace.[27]

In all the religious literature of classical Antiquity, there are few songs, with the exception of the sublime prayer of Cleanthes, where the religious emotion can be better felt regardless of whether the text is read in Greek or in the beautiful language of the French poet. Without any doubt the editorship of the poem dates from a rather late period, later in any case than the development of Stoic philosophy. But syncretism, reproduced in these songs, manifests itself from the very day upon which the Orphics rallied round the worship of Dionysus. In a fragment from Euripides, reproduced by Clement of Alexandria, one reads, 'To you, sublime administrator, I dedicate this libation; to you, Zeus or Hades, whichever name you choose . . . you are the one among the gods of heaven who holds the sceptre of Zeus; and you are also the one who shares the throne of Hades in the Underworld.'[28]

Orphic Eschatology

A necessary ancillary of this pantheistic philosophy is the concept that individual souls are temporarily separate parts of the All-Soul. Where the latter is the highest good, i.e. life in its plentitude, every separate, individual existence is harm, suffering, exile. Consequently, in order to gratify the sense of justice, imprisonment in a body can only be explained as a punishment or affliction. 'The followers of Orpheus', Plato makes Socrates say, 'give the name *σῆμα* [grave] to the punishment suffered by the soul to pay for its faults, and they regard the human body as a prison in which the soul is held.'[29]

Such a system necessarily implies belief, if not in a removal of the soul, then in the soul passing over to some other kind of situation. The circumstances of the present life are thought of as being the result of actions in a former existence; the actions in the present life determining the circumstances of the future and the future life in turn providing the souls 'which have fallen in life' the opportunity of wiping out or increasing their former blemishes;[30] and so on, until they have found their original purity again. The followers of Orpheus gave the human seed the name of *μίτος* (thread) and they compared the birth of a child with the knot of a net that reproduces in its meshes the sequence of individual situations of life.[31]

This cycle of rebirths, which are reminiscent of Indian concepts, can be followed on earth up the entire ascending ladder of animals and human beings, or it can take place in the world of stars which populate infinity, or—and here we are on mythological ground again—it could make use of the traditions related to the stay in Tartarus and the Elysian Fields. 'Musaeus and his son Eumolpus', relates Plato, 'distribute the just, rich rewards. They bring them, after death, to the home of Hades, and they allow them to sit, wreathed in flowers, at the banquet of the virtuous, where they live in everlasting intoxication. With respect to the wicked and the ungodly, they believe that these people will be banished to hell, plunged into a quagmire and condemned to carry water in a sieve.'[32]

Elsewhere Plato introduces the judges of the Underworld who pass sentences in which the punishment is proportional to the crime. What is quite distinct is that this reward after death has a definite character which cannot be reconciled with the principle of continual removal of the soul. Plato himself shows us that the souls from an animal body pass over to an astral or ethereal body depending on their conduct in each life.[33] The passage through Hades is no more than an intermediate purification. Pindarus is clearer on this point and it would certainly appear that he is reproducing Orphic ideas as he writes, 'Those from whom Persephone takes ransom for false steps in the past, will be sent back into the light by her after a period of nine years. This is the origin of great kings, men who are mighty through their power, or great through their wisdom and whom posterity will give the name of devoted heroes.'[34]

In a word, depending on whether the souls do good or bad, they will go either 'up' or 'down'. Should they debase themselves during their stay on earth, they will be exiled after death to the gloomy quagmires of Hades or even tortured by the torments which are so frighteningly depicted by the Mysteries. If, on the contrary, they become purer by freeing themselves of passions and lusts of the flesh, they will then come closer to their divine origin where they will find the bliss of which the Elysian Fields represents either a true picture or a symbol, depending on the initiates' mental attitude. This purification is the purpose of the 'Orphic Life', i.e. from an entire body of precepts, which aim at both the fulfilment of certain symbolic rites and the practice of modesty and virtue.[35] In this respect the followers of Orpheus are indeed the successors of Pythagoras.

Orphism and the Cult of Zagreus

Pausanias shows Onomacrites to be the writer of the *Passion of Dionysus* written in verse form.[36] Towards the end of the sixth century B.C. this god had already become, as we have seen, the symbol of Universal Life: he grows up, suffers, dies and is reborn in new circumstances. After the Orphics had taken over the Mysteries of Dionysus, Sabazios, Bacchus of Thrace and Phrygia, they appropriated the Mysteries of the Cretan Dionysus and it would even appear that they soon added those of Ida's Zeus and those of the Great Mother (Cybele). This is precisely what a chorus of bacchants sings in Euripides' *Cretans:*

> Purity has been the law of my life from the day when I was initiated into the Mysteries of Ida's Zeus; when I took part in the sacrifices according to the rule of Zagreus, the lover of nocturnal journeys, lit torches in honour of the Great Mother, and received the double name of Curetes and Bacchant. Clothed in pure white garments, I flee from the birth of mortals; I do not approach graves, and I do not tolerate in my food anything which has lived.[37]

Crete—the land where Hellenic concepts mingled with Asiatic religions and even with those of Egypt—had from earliest times a custom found among a certain number of wild barbaric tribes and which ethnologists consider to be a relic of totemism. The tribes which customarily refrain from eating certain animals because they hold them to be sacred, kill and eat precisely one of that same species on ceremonial occasions. Sometimes they cut the victim while still warm into pieces and dispute among themselves over the raw lumps. Robertson Smith, who has studied this form of sacrifice among the Semites, believes the explanation to be that, by eating the still fresh flesh and blood of a god, they draw a new flow of divine life into themselves.[38] It is probable that the earliest inhabitants of

Crete in a similar situation tore apart a bull after first conferring it with divine honour. At an unknown point in time, they identified this bull with the god Zagreus, and they invented or adopted a legend which explained how this ceremony represented the death of the god who was killed by the Titans.[39] It undoubtedly became the custom to keep the heart of the animal so as to sacrifice it to the local Zeus. This sacrifice is explained—perhaps under the influence of the Osiris legend which is connected with the phallus of the god killed by Typhon—by a suggestion that the heart of Zagreus was brought to Zeus so that the latter should give him a new body and life. Finally, Zagreus in turn was later identified with Dionysus. The latter was sometimes shown as a young man with the head of a bull or as a bull with theatrical shoes, and the sacrifice automatically received a place in the worship of the god of wine.[40]

The followers of Orpheus not only made Zagreus the god of universal destruction and renewal, a true demiourgos, recalling not only the Brahmin Siva, but also, in his capacity as the first-born (πϱωτόγονος) of Zeus, a kind of Logos, before Philo wrote about it. He manifested himself under all manner of names—he is the thousand-form Pan, the universal overlord (Παντοδυναστης). On the other hand, if he is the Great Hunter who catches men in his nets, as god of death, he is also the one who guarantees their immortality in his capacity as god of life and rebirth. In this way he justifies his name of Dionysus the Deliverer, the Saviour (Εωτήϱ). His opponents, the Titans, represent the confused powers and wicked passions which are temporarily victorious but which are finally conquered and punished. His glorification symbolizes the triumph of order in the universe. The myth adds that man was born from the ashes of the Titans who were destroyed by Zeus after they had delivered the divine child. In this way it is explained that man has a double nature: on the one hand titanic, demonic of which he must rid himself; on the other hand, divine which must be developed by continual exertion of the will. Even the animal sacrifice provided a means of sharing the life and immortality of the god by eating his flesh and blood.[41]

The great difference between the Mysteries of Dionysus Zagreus and those of Eleusis was originally that, in the former, the initiation was sufficient to obtain blessedness, whilst the initiate in the latter had to subject himself to a particular way of life—the Orphic life.

How Orphism Gained Admittance to Eleusis

It has been suggested that Orphism penetrated Eleusis by identifying Dionysus with Iacchus—the *archegetos* of the Mysteries, as described by Strabo—the divine leader of the procession who united the preceding purifications on Athenian territory with the Great Mysteries.[42] This procession, just as the person as Iacchus himself, unmentioned in the Homeric Hymn to Demeter, is first mentioned by Herodotus when referring to the second Persian war.[43] But there is nothing to show that Iacchus had ceased at this point in time to be the simple Demetrian spirit whose local origin is recalled by Strabo. A contrary hypothesis could even follow from the fact that in Aristophanes' *The Frogs*,[44] Dionysus meets the procession of Mystics apparently without the poet remarking on this duplication of the same person. But Euripides does state that the daughter of Demeter has to show special respect to the friends of Orpheus in the Underworld.[45] In addition, in his *Republic,* Plato makes Eumolpus the son of Musaeus[46] which shows that the followers of Orpheus had already succeeded in making a connection between their theology and the Eleusinian Mysteries. In the eyes of Aristophanes and Demosthenes, Orpheus is unquestionably the one who established the Mysteries.[47] We cannot therefore be very far from the truth if we place the penetration of Orphism in the Eleusinian Mysteries in the last years of the fifth or the beginning of the fourth century.[48]

How was this shown in his work? Suidas relates that the partisans of Orpheus, under the name of Eumolpus, had written a work consisting of three thousand lines of verse about the Mysteries of Demeter, about the adventures of the goddess with Celeos and about the initiation of his daughters.[49] But it is not likely that they completely changed the existing ceremonies. These were effectively recorded by the written and oral traditions of the Eumolpides. Even when they had yielded to Orphism, the Hierophant and the Daduchus would not have dared to change the outer form of the rites. The followers of Orpheus accomplished what the English Jacobites tried to do in the first half of the eighteenth century when they tried to introduce new degrees intended to unite the Stuart partisans into the existing Freemason organization in Great Britain. Orphism mainly used its new institution for a third level of initiation which followed the Great Mysteries: Epoptism.

It was probably then that Dionysus was identified with Iacchus.

By this amalgamation, Dionysus, who had already become one with Hades as husband of Cora, also became her brother as son of Demeter. On the other hand, Dionysus' identification with Zeus also made him Demeter's husband; he was thus consecutively linked with the daughter and the mother. He seems to have been finally represented as the son of Cora and Hades.[50]

This complex and even contradictory change of character by no means discouraged the followers of Orphism. They were never in better form than when it was a matter of creating profound truth from absurd contentions or some fine moral lesson from the most offensive images. So they would not have hesitated to introduce into Epoptism the sacrificing of animals or the mythological immortality which the early defenders of Christianity so strongly criticized in the Mysteries, and which even went against the grain with certain pagan authors.

The hierogamies, i.e. the representation of the more or less legal marriages between gods and goddesses, were not always of a lewd nature; for example the wedding of Zeus and Hera which was celebrated with all the formality of a legal marriage. In the drama of Demeter, it was the abduction of Cora and not the completion of the robbery which formed the principal episode. But in the Dionysian legend, which is presented in Epoptism, the voluntary or compulsory expressions of love are given a coarse, realistic character, which is not supported by the shape of animals or monsters assumed by the gods for this ceremony.[51] The spectators were not spared a single detail. At best the performance was cloaked in darkness when it reached the most offensive moments, just as certain writers prefer to put dots for decency's sake, while leaving the rest to the reader's imagination.[52] The actors of course only gave a sham performance. The author of *Philosophumena* even relates, perhaps ironically, that the Hierophants were given beforehand a drink made from hellebore on account of its anti-stimulation properties.[53] These performances, nevertheless, changed the hitherto sober, chaste traditions of the great Eleusinian goddesses.

Concerning the Dogmatic Education in the Mysteries

From the preceding remarks it seems that even if the supporters of Orphism had restricted themselves, in the Eleusinian Mysteries, to introducing the practices of the Dionysian cult, without also finding acceptance for their biology and ethics, one must conclude with Lobeck that their intervention had the single result of spoiling and lowering the ancient institution of the Mysteries. Many scholars now believe that these Mysteries, as a result, contain no kind of explanation of any philosophical or moral instruction. It was object teaching whereby each and every person attached whatever interpretation he fancied to the things he saw. In support of this proposition, two texts have been quoted, one from Plutarch, the other from Synesius. 'I listened to these things in all simplicity', writes the first, 'as in the initiation ceremonies which contain neither demonstration nor conviction which rest on reasoning.'[54] 'Aristotle', writes Synesius in turn, 'is of the opinion that the initiates learned nothing in any determined way; but that they received impressions; that they were led to a specific frame of mind for which they were properly prepared.'[55]

It should be hereby noted that Plutarch's text, in the general terms in which it is expressed, simply confirms the existence of ceremonies containing no explanations at all; but he by no means adds that these formed the whole initiation. With regard to Synesius, his second-hand opinion cannot exclude the existence of commentaries which may have preceded or followed the actual initiation. Clement of Alexandria informs us that the 'Small Mysteries contain a certain foundation of tuition and a preparation for everything which may follow.'[56] It is exactly what happens in the Christian liturgy, and particularly in the ceremonies of the Mass, in which the passion of Christ is symbolically performed. There too it is simply a matter of 'seeing and deepening nature and actions', but advance tuition has placed the believer in a position to understand the full meaning of the ceremony in the sense permitted by the theology of the church.

It is very likely that the instruction in Eleusis had the simple aim of making the candidates understand the legendary significance of the plays which would be enacted before their eyes, and to prepare them for the impressions spoken of by Synesius. Nevertheless, these explanations, whether given by the Hierophant himself or by the previously initiated mystagogues, provided the opportunity of orientating the explanation of the ceremonies towards a particular doctrine. Further instruction could and had to follow; that was undoubtedly the explanations expressed in the *hieros logos,* in which, according to Herodotus, the symbolism of the Mysteries was explained.[57] Galen mentions books which were intended only for the initiates.[58]

Mysteries other than those at Eleusis also consisted of purification ceremonies, symbolic displays, various dramas; but we know that they served as philosophical and moral instruction. As well as a natural explanation of the symbols and rites, there was also sometimes even a second, philosophical explanation, more subtle or deeper, only intended for the higher degrees. This seems to have been the case with the Mithraic Mysteries.[59]

The hieratic plays of the Great Mysteries and Epoptism were not merely pantomimes. The texts, collected by Foucart, very clearly indicate that the Hierophant accompanied the different parts of the performance with explanations.[60] These lessons even formed 'the' secrets. The orator Aristides gives sufficient proof of their importance when he writes with respect to Eleusis, 'Is there truly a place where what one sees emulates what actually happened?'[61] It is true that Foucart is of the opinion that they only consisted of passing on magic formulas, at the most a few explanations concerning the road to follow in the next world so as to reach the abode of the Chosen Ones. But there were also the Choruses, organized by the Hierophant and the Daduchus.[62] Authors speak of melodious songs which accompanied the radiant figures.[63] According to Eusebius, the fate of supernatural beings was shown 'according to ancient traditions and the secret doctrine by means of hymns and songs concerning the gods.'[64] In this manner too the Eleusinian priesthood was able to give the initiates instruction which was all the more effective because it formed to some degree part of the initiation ritual.

It is not difficult to establish that these liturgical songs were borrowed from the repertoire of Orphic hymns. Throughout the entire Roman domination, the Mysteries of Dionysus formed part of the Eleusinian liturgy. In his dissertation, *De Natura Deorum,* Cicero writes that the Mysteries were dedicated at one and the same time to Liber (Bacchus), Ceres and Libera (Proserpina).[65] Three centuries later a Latin inscription clearly explains that at Eleusis one was initiated through Bacchus, Ceres and Cora at the same time.[66] A passage from Pausanias shows us that the Orphic books had become the literature for the Mysteries. While he apologizes that he cannot explain why the candidates were not allowed to eat beans, he adds: 'Those who have seen the initiations of Eleusis, or have read the Orphic books, know what I mean.'[67] I should note here that these writings had, as a consequence, gained an esoteric character. A fragment of a hymn, reproduced by Eusebius, orders the door to be closed to the profane,[68] and Firmicus Maternus relates that an oath was administered to the initiates in the doctrine of Orpheus that they should impart nothing 'from the dread of revealing the secrets of the cult to profane ears.'[69] According to Suidas, there were in existence Dionysian commentaries (βακχικα ἑπιγϱάμμἀτα) relating to the Mysteries of Demeter; they were attributed to a woman follower of Pythagoras from Samos, Arignotea.[70]

It is even possible that as well as the dogma concerning divine wisdom, instruction in the Mysteries may have incorporated more direct moral lessons. H. Hieronymus writes that at the time of the philosopher Xenocrates one could still see in the Temple three of the laws attributed to Triptolemus: 'honour thy parents; worship the gods by offers of fruit; do not kill any living beings'.[71] The final precept moves us directly into Orphic life.

Plato refers to a speech from the Mysteries in which it was taught that man occupied a place which he was not permitted to leave.[72] In his commentary on the *Phaedo,* Olympiodorus says that the initiates pass through several degrees in order to approach morality and virtue (πολιτιλἀὶ ἀϱεταί).[73] Finally Seneca, making a comparison between the Mysteries and philosophy, leads us to understand that both of these institutions had a double form of instruction; one consisting of secrets, only intended for the initiates, the other of precepts which were also used amongst the profane.[74]

Indeed, only common sense could answer the question. Can one seriously accept that Plato, Cicero or Plutarch would have praised the moral influence of the Mysteries if they had merely found there a concept of the future life which was contradictory to their own ideal? Would the Athenian orator Andocides, four centuries before Christ, have said to his judges on pleading his own case before a tribunal of initiates: 'You have seen the *hiera* of both goddesses, so that you will punish the godless and save those who beware of wrong.'[75] If, as expressed by Diodorus, the neophytes returned from their initiation 'more devout, more righteous and in all ways better', they must have received instruction which was in accordance with the highest endeavours of their time; and there must have been something in these ceremonies other than empty symbols and magical rites.

Ethics versus Magic

But that does not mean that the Mysteries were never changed into a mere school of ethics or philosophy, a branch of the Academy or the Porticus. Orphism never ceased to represent material purifications as one of the principal elements of absolution and to attach a sacramental value to the symbolic actions of the initiation. Plato condemned the Orpheotelestai, those itinerant soothsayers who, basing themselves on books attributed to Orpheus and Musaeus, 'children of Selene and the Muses', went from door to door, offering to buy the sins of the whole family and even those of the ancestors against reasonable remuneration.[76] This religious materialism steadily increased in the last stages of paganism, at the time of the ram and bull sacrifices which penetrated as far as Eleusis. But should one judge an institution merely by those barterers in reliquaries and sellers of indulgence? The writings left to us by the followers of Orphism, even their concept of the Bacchic life, demonstrate that they thought of purification in moral terms, and it was this concept which gained the upper hand in the Mysteries, even when the externals of the Orphic rule of life, such as exclusively eating vegetarian food and wearing white clothing, fell into disuse or remained the privilege of a few philosophers.[77]

One may perhaps wonder how happiness in the life hereafter can be allowed to hang on two such different factors as the material execution of the rites and the observance of the ethical regimen. Again it is Egyptian religion which may provide us with the solution. The Egyptians had accepted the necessity of the formulas in the *Book of the Dead* to obtain help in reaching the fields of Ialou. They never deviated from this concept. But they added the idea of a tribunal which judged the deceased according to their merits and shortcomings. The 'double' of the guilty was then kept in the Underworld; that of the righteous was allowed to fight against the dangers and ambushes of the Underworld with the help of powerful magic formulas.

I do not personally believe in the direct influence of Egyptian religion, but the general manner of religious evolution has a universal bearing. Over the whole spectrum of religion, more is added than is changed. Where indeed can one find an ancient religion which has not demanded that ritual as well as moral precepts be among the conditions of admittance *sina qua non* to paradise?[78]

I should note here that a similar discrepancy is even revealed in the work of Plato. He sometimes leads us to believe that only the initiates will enjoy the company of the gods.[79] Elsewhere, on the contrary, as we have seen above, he gives the righteous the privilege after death of sitting at the divine banquet.

Philosophical Development in Eleusis

It is certain that from the time when Orphism obtained a foothold in the Mysteries, their development was a compromise between these two apparently contradictory elements: ethics, the importance of which increased as morals declined, and magic, which was given a fresh impulse by the influence of Eastern superstition. We must not forget that ethics for the people of Ancient times was never separate from either religion or philosophy. Creuzer's theory which made all Greek philosophy originate in the Mysteries, is simply an error in perspective. The immutability of the rites never hindered change in explanation; this always harmonized with the ideas of the most authoritative school in the different periods. This was a logical consequence of the circumstances, as Jean Réville so judiciously says: 'The Mysteries were intended to reveal the profound wisdom of the ancient legends; the priests therefore had to find in them whatever was considered to be the greatest wisdom according to the most respected philosophy.'[80] After Pythagorism which, together with Orphism must have gained entry into Eleusis, followed Stoicism in the century preceding the Roman conquest. If this were not so, one could never understand how Chrysippus could attribute to the Mysteries the merit of providing exact conceptions of the gods. Cicero also seems to be establishing the presence of Stoic doctrine when, in an allusion to the initiation ceremonies at Eleusis, Cotta says: 'The explanations which they contain, brought back to rationality, reveal the nature of things rather than that of the gods.'[81]

Seneca gives us the same impression when alluding to the Mysteries and an echo may be found in the judgement of Eusebius: 'The ancient knowledge of nature consists, amongst the Greeks as amongst the Barbarians, of conceptions concerning nature, concealed under the veil of the myth.' One can be convinced of it by the Orphic verses, and by the traditions of Egypt and Phrygia, but it is, above all, the orgiastic rites of the Mysteries and the symbolic actions of the initiation ceremonies which bring to light the ideas of the people of Ancient times.[82]

The principal revelation, however, must have been connected with the rewards in the life hereafter. In this respect, I have already quoted the evidence of Plato. Celsus explains that the Mysteries taught the doctrine of future rewards by examples from the fate of demons (i.e. of the souls of spirits) and Origen supported this view.[83] Plutarch, for his part, writes to his wife when comforting her on the death of their daughter, 'You will hear others claim that after the decomposition of the body, there is no more good, bad or sorrow. That is a doctrine from which I know you are protected, both by the principles which you inherited from your forefathers and by the sacred symbols used in the Mysteries of Dionysus.'[84]

If one may believe St Augustine, Varro saw in the Eleusinian Mysteries exclusively an allusion to the development of the grain; in any case he claimed that many of its features were purely connected with agriculture.[85]

This is precisely the rational explanation which belonged to Stoic doctrine. But Varro's assertion strengthens our suspicions that a deeper philosophical doctrine existed as, indeed, in the Orphic view. Otherwise the Mysteries would have no other purpose and no other result than that of displaying their own meaninglessness. The Stoics applied themselves to laying the foundations of morality on logic rather than on the prospect of reward or punishment in the life hereafter. The Alexandrian school, which succeeded Stoicism in Eleusis, laid the emphasis on the eschatological side of the Mysteries; and there is no reason to doubt that there, as elsewhere, the Neo-Platonists and the Neo-Pythagoreans endeavoured to bring the maintenance and even the re-institution of the traditional ceremonies into line with the most elevated concepts achieved by philosophy and ethics in their time. In order to attain this goal, they merely had to follow the trail laid by Orphism. Quite apart from the Orphic works of this period which reflect the ideas of the Alexandrians, the writings of Porphyros and Proclus give sufficient proof that Neo-Platonism had become the philosophy of the Mysteries. Maximus, Eunapus, Julianus and undoubtedly Proclus were Eleusinian initiates and the function of the Hierophant was, in the fourth and fifth centuries A.D., more than once filled by Neo-

Platonist philosophers.[86] Never, perhaps, was there such a close connection between religion and philosophy.

The Climax and Destruction of Eleusis

The disappearance of the intellectual and religious horizon, with the conquest of Alexander, had caused, in the entire Greek world, the development of pantheism, with its origin in the mixture of different systems. On the one hand, this pantheism tended to compare the principal gods of the various known systems; on the other hand, it tended to make from these gods the representatives of one single god—the essential soul of the world. We have seen that Orphism, of which Eleusis had become the centre, had set the example for this double system. One can therefore appreciate the increasing power of attraction which the Mysteries of Eleusis exercised wherever Hellenic civilization penetrated. Immediately after the death of Alexander, when Ptolemy Soter, following his ascendancy to the throne of the Pharaohs, wished to unite the Egyptian and Greek religions, it was a Eumolpides, named Timotheus, whom he summoned from Eleusis to Alexandria to exercise the function of elucidating the texts.[87]

Under Roman rule, this popularity increased. Rome accepted the Mysteries of Eleusis just as it had accepted the other religious institutions of Greece, and Cicero tells us of the high regard they enjoyed amongst the most educated people in the Republic. The Empire first seemed to want to keep only the ancient Roman religion; but this reaction could not hold its own against the invasion of Eastern religions. In the second century A.D., all public religions from the basin of the Mediterranean had accepted pantheistic mythology which bore clear traces of having been cast in the mould of Alexandrian metaphysics, and, to justify retention of their special rites, they tried to explain them within the framework of those metaphysical systems by means of initiations, more or less moulded according to the example of those in Eleusis.

If one investigates the trends which dominated the last period of ancient paganism, one can establish that, not only was there a belief in an abstract God, who became more and more elusive, but there was also a search for intermediary beings who could solve the problem of creation and also answer the practical requirements of religious feeling. Equally, there was a desire to retain the old cults by linking them through symbolism to prevailing ideas, and there was an intense need for establishing a system of purification and redemption and, at the same time, a childish belief in the efficiency of magical formulas and ceremonies. These were precisely the desires which the Mysteries could guarantee to satisfy.

The restless spirits endlessly moved from one initiation to the other. Apulaeus relates that he became an initiate of most of the Mysteries of Greece, adding that there was nothing abnormal about this.[88]

In his *Saturnalia,* Macrobius portrays a Roman lady who has been initiated into the Mysteries of Demeter and Cora, Dionysus, Hecate and Isis; her husband, Praetextatus, was *pater patrum* in the Mysteries of Mithras, high priest of Vesta and of Isis. The number of initiation centres had considerably expanded; but Eleusis still held the first place. Only the Mysteries of Mithras seem to have disputed the spiritual leadership of the pagan community with the Mysteries of the great goddesses, which were followed by the formation of those of Dionysus. But not withstanding the favour in which sun worship was held by the last pagan emperors, the Mithras cult was never so completely accepted by Greek civilization as the Eleusinian cult.[89] Mithras always remained a barbarian God, whereas the Eleusinian Mysteries never ceased to represent, for the enlightened spirits, all which was most exalted in the classical tradition. 'As high as the Greeks are above the heroes', relates Pausanias, 'so are the Eleusinian Mysteries above the other institutions connected with worship of the gods.'[90]

When Julianus seems to find some difficulty in comprehending a philosophical doctrine, he turns to the high priest of Eleusis for help.[91] So great was the popularity or, if you wish, the respectability of the Mysteries that they were still openly celebrated with all the splendour of former times, throughout the half century which followed the death of Constantine, even after Gratius and Theodosius had ordered the confiscation of the temple furnishings and had forbidden ceremonies of pagan worship, whereas in Rome the sanctuaries of Mithras were plundered and closed.

There can be no doubt about the end. The Christian apologists had well and truly struck their opponent's weak point when they incessantly hammered away at the argument, formulated as follows by Gregory of Nazianza: 'In our religion, you will not find that a Cora is abducted, a Demeter is wandering around or a Celeos and a Triptolemus are represented by snakes etc.'[92] Viewed from the philosophical and moral standpoint, the Mysteries contain doctrines which were perhaps as lofty as those of Christianity but which merely hastened their fall. Jean Réville pinpointed it exactly when he demonstrated that the greatest blossoming of the community of Antiquity had invoked a new ideal in life:

> The heroism of the sanctity, the rebirth, the blessedness through the purity of heart, already beginning here below, to be continued in the life hereafter; the universal fraternity reaching beyond social position and nationality; the care for those inferior or the oppressed; the desire for progress and spiritual fulfilment; the thirst for living communion with the gods; the worship of the great incarnations of the divine in history.

But he is no less right when he demonstrates that the reformers who were striving for a mixture of the systems were in this way working for the Gospel.[93] From the moment when a number of the Neo-Platonists in Alexandria went with bag and baggage over to the camp of the young church, the fall of paganism was simply a question of years.

Eleusis did not see its Mysteries done away with by an imperial decree, nor was it desecrated by its former followers. The end was more tragic. Under Gallias, a high priest of Eleusis had repulsed an attack of Goths who threatened the sacred city.[94] In A.D. 396 the Goths again appeared in Attica, led by Alaric, and the monks, who had gained enough influence over the usurper to make him spare Athens, undoubtedly easily persuaded him that he could harmlessly enter the sanctuary of the good goddesses which was then plundered and burnt.[95] In modern times, under the charred remains of the Propylaea, the body of a Goth was excavated, recognizable by his armour; he had died as the building collapsed upon him[96]—a barbarian buried under the collapse of a world. Eleusis had once already been destroyed and burnt by the Persians, after the battle of Plataea. The Athenians immediately rebuilt an even greater and more beautiful sanctuary. After the passage of Alaric, no one thought of rebuilding the ruins. But the rites were not completely lost.

[1]*Schol. ad Aristoph.,* Plut. line 1013.
[2]Diodorus IV, 14, 3.
[3]See the interesting study in which Dumoulin has collected all classical texts which relate to Epimenides. ('Epimenide de Crète' in the *Annals of the Faculty of Lit. and Philos. of the Univ. of Liège,* Liège 1891).
[4]Pausanias I, 14, 3.

[5]Plutarch, *De Cupid. Divit.*, VIII (Didot), III, p. 638.
[6]Decharme, *Mythol. de la Grèce Ant.*, p. 446.
[7]Herodotus V, 67.
[8]Maury, *Rel. de la Grèce,* III, p. 327.
[9]*Etymologicon Graec. ling. Gudianum,* under the word Ζαγϱέυς—It seems impossible to put the editorship of the *Alcmeonides* later than the seventh century B.C. Some academics even allow it to climb still higher. But is it certain that this rule is not an Orphic insertion?
[10]Plutarch, *De Ei, ap. Delph.,* 9 (389b).
[11]One of the few human sacrifices which Ancient Greece has had to recognize is the killing by Themistocles in 480 B.C. of three young men in honour of Dionysus Omestes (Plutarch, *Themistocles,* 13).
[12]Plutarch, *De Ei apud Delph.,* 9.
[13]For the attributes of Dionysus and the features of his cult see Gerhard, *Griech. Myth.;* Maury, *Myth. de la Grèce Antique,* I, p. 510 and following; especially Lenormant, *Daremberg and Saglio,* I, p. 591 and following.
[14]The Orphic movement still forms one of the least studied chapters in the history of Greek thought. While awaiting the publication of *Orphica,* promised by Dietrich and Kroll, we must refer for texts to the second part of the *Aglaophamus* of Lobeck and to the *Orphica* of Hermann (Leipzig, 1805), Abel (Leipzig, 1885) and Dietrich (Marburg, 1891); and for commentaries to the works of Alfred Maury concerning the 'Cosmogènies Orphiques' in the *Revue Archéologique* (part VII). We may also refer to Jules Girard on *Le Sentiment Religieux en Grèce* (Paris, 1st edn., 1869) and to Gruppe in the *Lexicon der Mythologie* by Röscher (article, 'Orpheus'). One should also add the work of Maas, *Orpheus* (Munich, 1895) in which the writer does his utmost to trace Orphic influence both in Greek and Roman cults and in early Christianity.
[15]In some systems this 'second god' is split into several beings which personify the successive actions of creation and form, so to speak, a new polytheism. The Demiourgos and the Cosmos of Numenius divide into: the Good (*το καλον*); the Mind (*ὁ νοῦς*); the Soul (*ηψυχῄ*) of Plotinus; the chain of gnostic aeons, etc. But however numerous they may seem, these beings arise from absolute reality and once more fuse into one.
[16]These songs have been translated into English by Thomas Taylor (*The Mystic Hymns of Orpheus,* Chiswick, 1824) and into French by Leconte de Lisle (Paris, 1869).
[17]Sextus Empiricus, *Hypotyp.,* III, 4 (1621), p. 115. See also Ausones, *Griphus,* line 74, where the three gateways of the Orphic tripod represent earth, water and fire.
[18]'I know then', says Plutarch 'that there exist first of all four roots of all things: Brilliant Zeus; Hera; Hades, the maintainer; and Nestis whose tears feed the springs.' (*De placit philos.,* 1, 30).
[19]The Ocean and its sister Thetis (Plato, *Cratyle,* XIX).
[20]See Cumont, *Mithra,* I pp. 78 and 294. Although James Darmesteter amply took into account the influence of Greek philosophy in the development of Mazdean theology, he recognizes that 'it is not impossible that Zervanism already existed under the Achemenides, because the dogma of the finite duration of the world supposes that of infinite time.' Statement of the 'Zend. Avesta' in the 24th part of

the *Annals of the Guimet Museum* (1893), p. 70.
[21]Simplicius, *Ad Auscult,* I, 31, 6.
[22]Proclus, *Cratyl.*. p. 13.
[23]'Ο μὲν δὴ Θεός, ὥσπερ καὶ ὁ παλαιὸς λόγος, ἀρχήν τε καὶ τελευτὴν και μερα των ὄντων ἁ πάντωγ ἔχων. Plato, *Leges* IV, Didot, p. 326.
[24]Max Muller, *Origines et developpement de la religion,* transl. by Darmesteter (Paris, 1879), p. 237.
[25]'Αρρήτοις λέκτροίσι τεκνωθεις (Hymn XXX, 2, Hymn XXIX, 7: ἀρρήτονσι γοναις).
[26]Macrobe, *Saturn,* I, ch. 18.
[27]Hymn IX (X in the translation of Leconte de Lisle).
[28]Clement of Alexandria, *Stromat.* V, 12, 71. Most scholars believe that this fragment comes from the 'Cretans'; see *Eurip. Fragmenta* (Didot), frg. 966.
[29]*Cratyle* XVII.
[30]See what Empedocles says in Plutarch, *De Exilio,* 17: 'I am now also one of the exiles who wander around far from God, because they have listened to angry discord.'
[31]Maury, *Rel. de la Grèce,* III, p. 313.
[32]*De Republ.,* II, (Didot), p. 26.
[33]*De Rep.,* X (Didot), p. 456.
[34]Pindarus, fragm. XVI, 98.
[35]Palto, *Leges,* VI (Didot), p. 371.
[36]Pausanias, VIII, 37, 3.
[37]Fragm. in Porphyry, *De Abstinentia,* IV, 19.
[38]Robertson Smith, *Religion of the Semites,* p. 282 and following.
[39]Frazer wonders if one should not seek a similar custom in the origin of the myth of Osiris who was killed by Typhon; *The Golden Bough,* part I, p. 306.
[40]The animal which was torn apart alive in the Bacchanalia was not always a bull but sometimes a goat as can be seen in the paintings on various antique vases (*Musée de Sculpture,* pl. 126, No. 118; 135, No. 118); especially on a vase which is now in the British Museum (*Panofka Musée Blacas,* pl. 13).
[41]Girard, *Du sentiment religieux en Grèce,* p. 26.
[42]Strabo, lib. IX, ch. 1.
[43]Herodotus, *Hist.* VIII, 65.
[44]*Ranae,* line 324 and following.
[45]τούς 'Ορφέως τιμωσα φαινεσθαι φίλους, Euripìdes, *Rhesos,* line 965 (Didot), p. 363. See also lines 943-4.
[46]Plato, *The Republic,* lib. II.
[47]Aristophanes, *Ranae,* line 1032: 'Ορφεύς μὲν γαρ τελετας Θ'ήμιν κατεδειξε, φονων τ'ἀπεχεσται; Demosthenes, *Advers. Aristogiton* I, 172, 26: 'Οτας ἁγιωτατας ἡμιν τελετας καταδειξας 'Ορφεως.
[48]Lenormant himself thought the exact date could be fixed at 380 B.C., when the function of the Daduchus was passed on to the branch of the Lycomides when the Kerykes died out. The Lycomides held Mysteries in Phlya similar to those of Eleusis. According to Pausanias (IX, 27, 2; I, 22, 7) Hymns attributed to Orpheus, Musaeus and Pamphos were sung in honour of Demeter. But Foucart has demonstrated that in all probability, the function of Daduchus remained in the family of the Kerykes (*Recherches,* 2nd review, pp. 47-48).

[49]*Lexicon,* under the word Εὔμολπος.
[50]See in the *Dict. de Daremberg et Saglio* the article devoted to Bacchus by F. Lenormant (part I, p. 632-6).
[51]Zeus marries in turn Demeter in the form of a bull and their daughter Cora in the form of a snake or a dragon.
[52]Diodorus of Sicily says that the worship of Dionysus Sabazios was held at night and in secret because decency demanded that the secret of the sexual relationship be veiled (IV, 4, 1).
[53]*Philosophumena,* lib. V, 1. 171, (Migne), p. 3149.
[54]Plutarch, *De Defect. Oracul.,* ch. 22.
[55]Synesius, *Oration,* Petau, p. 48.
[56]'It is not without reason that in the Greek Mysteries purification first took place in a way, similar to the washing of the barbarians. Then follow the Small Mysteries which include a certain amount of fundamental instruction and preparation for everything which follows. With respect to the Great Mysteries, in their totality there is nothing more to learn here; one can merely watch and go deeper into nature and actions.' (*ἐποπτεὐειν δἑ καὶ περινεύειν τήν φυσιν και τὰ πράγματα.*) *Stromat* V, (Bekker), p. 682.
[57]Herodotus, lib. II, 48, 62, 81.
[58]'Some have dared to read the Mystery books without being initiated.' *De simpl. medic.,* VII, ch. 1, quoted by Maury, *Rel. de la Grèce,* II, p. 137.
[59]Cumont, *Mystères de Mithra,* part I, p. 73. Prophyry informs us that the initiation ceremonies for the different Mithraic degrees were symbolic allusions to the signs of the Zodiac, but he adds that in reality they were connected with the destiny of the soul after death. (*De Abstinentia,* IV, 16).
[60]Foucart, *Recherches* (1st review, p. 59 and following).
[61]Aristides, *Eleusin.,* p. 256.
[62]Philostratus, *Vitae Sophist.,* II, (Didot), p. 252.
[63]Plutarch, *Ex Opere de Anima,* II, 6; Justin Martyr, *Cohort Adgentes,* 38; Themistius, *Orat.,* XX.
[64]Eusebius, *Praefarat. evang.,* lib. III, Provem. I.
[65]*De nat. Deor.,* lib. II, 24.
[66]*Sacrata apud Eleusinam deo Baccho, Cereri et Corae,* C.I.L., part VI, No. 1780.
[67]Pausanias I, 37, 4.
[68]Eusebius, *Praeparat., evang.,* lib. XIII, ch. 12.
[69]Firmicus Maternus, *Mathesis* VII, (Basel, 1532), p. 193.
[70]Suidas, *Lexicon,* 'Αριγνώτη.
[71]Γονεις τιμᾶν Θεούς κάρποις ἀγάλλειν, ξῶά μὴ σινεσθαι, H. Hieronymus, *Adv. Jovinian.,* lib. II, ch. 9 (Antwerp, 1529), p. 169.
[72]*Phaedo* VI.
[73]*Commentaire du Phédon,* quoted by de Sacy (in the work by Sainte-Croix, *Recherches sur les Mystères du Paganisme* (Paris, 1817), I, p. 422).
[74]Seneca, *Epist.,* XCV. 'Sicut sanctiora sacrorum tantum initiati sciunt, ita in philosophia arcana illa admissis receptisque in sacra ostenduntur; at praecepta et ilia eiusmodi profanis quoque nota sunt.'
[75]Andocides, *De Mysteriis,* 31, (Didot), p. 53.
[76]Plato, *De republ.,* II, (Didot), p. 27.
[77]In the third century A.D., it may have been possible to differentiate Orphic life

from Pythagorean life, as practised by the Neo-Pythagoreans of that time. See Philostrates, *Vita Apollon.* (Teubner, Lipsae, 1870), 1, 2, 7, 8, 13, 32.

[78]The same phenomenon may be noted in Buddhism which also seeks salvation in a life of purity and denial, comparable to Orphic life, but, particularly amongst the northern Buddhists, for whom the attaintment of Nirvana depends on the fulfilment of magical practices inherited from Hinduism (see Louis de la Vallée, 'Bouddhisme: Etudes et Matériaux', in the part 55 of the *Mém. Couronm. de l'Acad. Roy. de Belgique,* p. 87 and following.).

[79]*Phaedo,* XIII, XXIX.

[80]*La Religion à Rome sous les Sévères* (Paris, 1886), p. 178.

[81]Quibus explicatis ad rationemque revertis, rerum magis natura cognoscitur quam deorum.' (*De Natura Deor.* I, 42). In another treatise (*Tusuculan.* I, 13) Cicero appears to accept that the doctrine of the Mysteries resembled Ephemerism. In reality Epicurism is the only one of the principal philosophical systems of classical Greece which was irreconcilable with Orphic tradition. In the imitation of the Mysteries by Alexander the Paphlagonian, the latter begins by heralding the exclusion of the deniers of god, i.e. the Epicureans and the Christians. (Lucien, *Alexandr.,* 38).

[82]Eusebius, *Praepar. Evang.,* lib. III, Proemium.

[83]Origen, *In Cels.,* lib. VIII, ch. 48.

[84]Plutarch, *Consol, ad uscor,* X.

[85]'Varro de Eleusiniis nihil interpretatur nisi quod attinet ad frumentum . . . Dici deinde multa in mysteriis tradiquae non nisi ad frugum inventionem pertineant.' *De Civit. Dei,* II, 20.

[86]Eunapus, *Vita Maxim.,* (Didot), p. 376; Philostrates, *Vitae Sophist.,* II, 20, p. 752.

[87]Plutarch, *De Isid. et Osixid.,* XXVIII. In Tacitus, Timotheus bears the title of 'antistites caeremoniarum'. (*Hist.* IV, 83).

[88]'Sacrorum pleraque initia in Graecia participavi; nihil insolitum, nihil incognitum dico? Apulaeus, *Apolog.* (Didot), p. 235.

[89]Lucius names Mithras, along with Sabazios and Attis, among the barbarian gods whose admittance to Olympus was deeply regretted by the Greek gods (*Deorum Concil.,* ch. 9). When Origen reproaches Celsus for seeking arguments against Christianity in the Mithraic Mysteries, he adds, 'I do not truly believe that the Mysteries of Mithras are more highly respected by the Greeks than those of Eleusis or those who are celebrated in Aegina in honour of Hecate.' (*Contra Cels.,* lib. VI, 647, Migne).

[90]Pausanias X, 31, 11.

[91]Eunapus, *Vita Maxim.,* (Didot), p. 475.

[92]Gregory of Nazianza, *Orat.,* XXXIX, 4.

[93]Jean Réville, *La Religion sous les Sévères,* p. 298 and following.

[94]*Corp. Insc. Graec.,* No. 401.

[95]Eunapus, *Vit. Maxim.* (Didot), p. 476.

[96]F. Lenormant, *Revue de l'Architecture* (Paris, 1868), p. 14.

CHAPTER 5
WHAT HAS SURVIVED OF THE MYSTERIES?

All Mysteries of the Ancient classical world had the original purpose of bringing the initiate into communication with certain divine beings, with the aim of providing him with the benefits which these gods were reputed to have at their disposal.

When the progressive intermingling of systems had sealed the equality of the gods and the mutual transfer of their attributes, there was no further reason why ceremonies which could exercise influence on certain supernatural beings could not be considered to have a similar influence on all. The ceremonies of the Mysteries had indeed never ceased to possess an inner value, like all rites of a magical origin. Once their special connection with this or that particular form of worship was broken, they could be used on more or less all occasions when the intermediary of a supernatural power had to be invoked. The last periods of paganism show a *rapprochement* with the ceremonies and doctrines of the principal Mysteries.

In the partly veiled story of his initiation into the Mysteries of Isis, Apulaeus makes use of images which recall the plays at Eleusis. 'I have advanced as far as the boundaries of death, and, after disturbing the threshold of Proserpina, I returned thence through the elements. At midnight, I saw the sun shine in its full beauty. I have approached the gods of hell and the gods of heaven.'[1] A tomb in the Roman catacombs has for a long time attracted the attention of archaeologists. It bears paintings and inscriptions which suggest a harmonious blending of the Mysteries of Cora, Sabazios and perhaps Mithras. They show a dead woman, Vibia, being led to the Underworld by Hermes; she is brought into the presence of Dis Pater and Abra Cura i.e. Hades and Persephone; finally, following a favourable judgement, she is led by her good genius to the banquet of the righteous[2]

I have already shown how Eleusis itself in the time of Cicero had closely blended the Mysteries of Dionysus with those of the Great Goddesses. The fragmentary descriptions which the Christian writers of the fourth century dedicate to the pagan initiations often make us doubt whether their innuendoes relate to the Mysteries of Demeter and Cora, of Dionysus, Attis, Cybele or the Cabiri. Recently in Eleusis the existence has been established of a cave or pit which seems to have been used for the sacrifices of bulls which were a feature of the Mysteries of Cybele[3] There is therefore no reason to be surprised when we see that in the second half of the fourth century A.D., when the Eumolpides family had died out, a high priest of Mithras was sought abroad to be made Hierophant of Eleusis[4]

Did this mutual exchange also extend to the Christian communities which were formed on Graeco-Roman ground at the time of extinction of this ancient society? For a long time people have searched exclusively in Judea for not only the early origin of Christian religious doctrine but also its organization and its worship. The progress of historical criticism has led one to believe that it is impossible to explain the development of Christian institutions in the Graeco-Latin world if one persists in leaving out the influence of pagan philosophies and cults.

It is superfluous to recall the famous work in which Ernest Renan has outlined, with as much exegetic acumen as literary merit, the part played by both ethnic currents in the formation of the Church. After the works of the school of Baur, we have had the works of the two masters in Christian exegesis: Adolphe Harnack and Edwin Hatch. Harnack demonstrated, to use his own expressions, how 'dogmatic Christianity, the dogmas in their conception and composition, are the work of the Greek spirit on evangelical ground,'[5] and Hatch extended this evidence to the organization and ceremonies of the Christian communities on Greek soil.[6] The connection between Christian liturgy and pagan cults have, in recent years, been the subject of important monographs, particularly those of Anrich and Wobbermin.[7] These works make it possible for me to pass more quickly over certain sections of the problem.

The method to be followed is clearly given by Edwin Hatch:

1. Establish the nature of Christian religion before and after its contact with Hellenism.
2. Ascertain if, amongst the new elements which appear as a consequence of that contact, there are also those found in the Mysteries.
3. Investigate if these elements could have had their origin in some other source.

The Mysteries and Gnosticism

As often occurs in times of transition, the first centuries of Christianity saw the revival of sects which wanted to link the new cult to its predecessors. These attempts emanate particularly from Graeco-Syrian and Alexandrian quarters. Emperor Hadrian wrote from Alexandria deriding the religious fickleness of his Egyptian subjects: 'Here you see Christians worshipping Serapis, and worshippers of Serapis who call themselves bishops of Christ.'[8] They were apparently Gnostic Christians, half pagan like the sects, whom Origen and Plotinus, the apologists of the Church and the Neo-Platonist doctors contested at the same time.[9] Some critics claim that the Gnostics of the second century pursued Orphism.[10] The proposition gains greater authority if one accepts, as I have already claimed, that Orphism was more of a method than a doctrine. And indeed Gnosticism shows an entirely Orphic tendency to amalgamate, under the cover of belief in a beatific god, the principal theological systems which had developed in the former polytheism through contact with Neo-Platonic theory.

The Gnostics were connected with Neo-Platonism in that, after establishing the reality and the inscrutability of the First Principle, they developed from this secret source a series of worlds which ended with the world of matter, and using that they explained this gradual descent of the creative power into matter by a fault or false step of the intermediate powers. They belonged to Christianity in that they attributed to the divine spark, confined in man, the ability to arise again to the Pleroma or the higher world, thanks to the intervention of a charitable son, Christ, descended in the person of Jesus, to spread the liberating Gnosis among people.

Most Gnostic sects divided mankind into three parts: the material, the psychic or initiates in the lowest degree; and the pneumatists, who alone received the full revelation. Some, such as the Carpocrations, believed that possessing the Gnosis was sufficient to ensure salvation and even, if one can believe opponents, release from all religious and moral laws. But in the eyes of others, and these were the most numerous sects, certain theurgic ceremonies had to be added, such as baptism, which formed the actual initiation, and the Holy Communion which brought about union with the higher powers. Before receiving baptism, one had to swear not to impart anything about the Mysteries which one was about to learn.[11] A few schools multiplied the number of initiation degrees. Apart from baptism, the initiation ceremony also included the laying on of hands; marking with a seal (σφϱαγίϱ); anointing, perhaps introduced into Christianity by the Gnostics; recitation of formulas with a double meaning, as in the pagan Mysteries; and, finally, the display of sacred symbols and the explanation of symbolic representations, such as the diagram of the Ophites, described by Origen.[12]

Two Coptic manuscripts of Valentinian origin, discovered quite recently in the East, the Pistis Sophia and the Oxford papyrus, called the *Book of the Great Logos* according to the Mystery, give in detail four consecutive initiation scenes: baptism by water 'which gives admittance to the region of Truth and the region of Light'; baptism by fire 'which gives a place amongst the inheritors of the Kingdom of Light'; spiritual baptism; finally the 'Mystery' which constrains all Archones to take away the sins of the disciples, making the latter immortal.[13] The concept that sacraments as such, and especially baptism, have power, and morally change the believer, seems to have appeared amongst the Gnostics before they were admitted to the orthodox communities.[14] Simon Magus, who is considered to be the founder of Gnosticism, and his successor Menander, were already teaching that baptism ensured immortality.[15] Others limited themselves to assuming that it wiped out all former sins; it was more likely to have been the Communion which gave eternal life.

The purpose of Gnosticism is exclusively aimed at the life hereafter, it was a matter of ensuring the return of the individual soul to the pleroma, or at least admittance to the ogdoad, which formed the intermediate world. According to 'Extracts from Theodotus' which expresses the Valentinian tradition of the East, the spirits in the ogdoad take part in an eternal banquet, recalling the Banquet of the Righteous of Plato. Also, 'the pneumatists . . . will have the angels as their spouses . . . they will enter the bridal room of the ogdoad in the presence of the spirit; they will become sympathetic aeons; they will participate in spiritual and eternal weddings.'[16] The Valentinian baptistry was consequently called Νυμφών or 'Bridal room'.[17] This is an expression which, however spiritually, strongly recalls the 'bridal bed' (παοτός) of Eleusinian Epoptism.[18] One should not then be so surprised when Tertullian, with the prejudiced exaggeration which characterizes all his attacks, accuses the Valentinians of having imitated the Eleusinian Mysteries and even of 'having engaged them into lewdness'.[19]

Another head of the Gnostic school, Bardesanus, even went as far as to promise the pneumatists marriage with Sophia, the heavenly spirit of Christ.[20] It is the same mystical concept which made the Greek initiates husbands of Persephone after their death.[21] It is generally agreed that more credence can be attached to the information provided by the writer of the *Philosophumena* with respect to the Gnostics than to the claims of the other apologists. This work relates that the Sethianians, a sect related to the Ophites, had borrowed their doctrines from the Gnostics and their ceremonies from the Mysteries of Phlya, where, as we have already seen, they used a ritual similar to that of Eleusis.[22] With respect to the Ophites themselves, the *Philosophumena* demonstrates that they had adopted the principal rites of the Epoptea of Eleusis, by making them subservient to the symbolizing of their own theories concerning the origin and the destination of the soul.

They went so far that they even explained the name Eleusis as the 'descent' (from 'ελεύσεσθαυ, ἐλθετν meaning 'to come' or 'to move') with the allusion to the fate of the spirits which were cast down from the higher world.[23]

Other authors inform us that the Ophites kept tame snakes in their temples. These reptiles came out of their basket at the celebration of Communion and wound themselves around the consecrated bread.[24] It is a performance that makes one think of certain Greek vases on which one can see the sacred snakes of Demeter or Dionysus lifting the lid of their basket so as to approach the initiates. With respect to the mythical snake which gave its name to the sect, the Ophites saw in it either the true form or at least a symbol of their Demiourgos; some illustrations of it found on Cabbalistic stones strongly recall the Orphic description of Phanes in the shape of a winged serpent with three heads: that of a dragon, a bull and a lion.[25]

Gnosticism did not only borrow its symbols from the Mysteries of Eleusis. Its views about the fate of the soul which, either in its descent to the earth or its ascent to the pleroma, had to pass through the spheres of seven planets, passage through which had to be requested from the spirits or aeons who ruled those planets, resemble too closely the Chaldean Persian world-view of the Mithras Mysteries for this not to have had an influence on the ritual of sects who claimed to link the revelations of Zoroaster with those of Jesus and Orpheus. It is also important to point out that the Gnostic movement was increasingly influenced by Manichaeism.

The Manichaeans also had their secret doctrine and their initiations—especially the *Consolamentum,* whereby one's commitment to the Holy Ghost was given by the laying on of hands. Their symbolism, however, like that of the later sects grafted on to the same stem, indicates an Eastern rather than Greek origin, as one would have expected. It is through another channel that certain Eleusinian ceremonies have reached us.

The Mysteries and Christianity

There are fortunately in existence documents which permit us to reconstruct the principal steps of liturgical evolution in the Church between the apostolic era and the triumph of Christianity in the fourth century. Among the documents concerning the first Christian communities, furnished by the Acts of the Apostles and the Letters of Paul, we can add from the beginning of the second century the Didache,[26] at least for the Graeco-Syrian communities, and a little later the Apology of Justin the Martyr; those of Clement of Alexandria and Origen, the apostolic laws; and, as our final point, the official liturgies which are believed to date back to the fourth and fifth centuries, such as the *Catechism* of Cyril of Jerusalem, the Liturgy of Jacob, the Ambrosian, Gregorian and Leontine prayer books etc.

This task is considerably facilitated by the learned, painstaking work of Duchesne concerning the origin of Christian religious practice.[27]

It has sometimes been claimed that Jesus had a double doctrine: the one exoteric for the great majority of followers; the other esoteric, for the Apostles who would have been especially charged with it, to ensure the survival of the secret dogma, pending the day when it could be made known without danger. This theory which, already proclaimed by Valentine and other Gnostics and which still found defendants in the nineteenth century,[28] has now been completely abandoned.[29] If there is any kind of firm historical truth it is that the Christian religion at its conception had nothing secretive about it. It was accessible to all who accepted Christ as the Messiah. The few admission prerequisites were exclusively moral. In the third century, however, Christianity became a Mystery in the Greek sense of the word, with a complicated ritual which included a sacramental initiation and this character particularly comes to the fore in the communities which have the most contact with Alexandrian culture. What was the origin of these new elements?

Christianity and Vocabulary of the Mysteries

The Apostle Paul was already using the expressions *μύστηϱιον* and *τέλειος* respectively to indicate the divine revelation and the perfect Christian. The Neo-Platonic Christians of Alexandria and, in general, the church writers of the third to the fifth centuries, make even more frequent use of such expressions by applying Eleusinian vocabulary to the new religion. 'O, eternally sacred Mysteries!' writes Clement of Alexandria, 'I became holy through initiation. The Lord is the high priest; he imprinted his seal on the Mystic when he granted him enlightenment;[30] he places those who are believers and remain eternally in his care, in the hands of his Father. See here the spiritual ecstasy of our Mysteries, if you will. Be initiated and you will dance in the chorus of Angels, around the uncreated God, the Undying, the only true Being, while the divine Logos sings the holy hymn with us.' The bishop who leads the ceremony assumes the name of 'Mystagogue', and the neophyte, following baptism, that of 'initiate', '*teleios*', 'Mystic' (*τέλειος, μυεηθις, μυσταγωγουμενος*) or 'Enlightened One' (*φωτισθείς*) and sealed (*'εσφϱα γιφμένος*).[30] The profane (the unbaptized) are referred to by the same name as in the time when the hymn to Demeter was composed, i.e. 'αμυήτοι'[31] The priest is the one who brings enlightenment, (φωυοτικος). The communion becomes a sacrifice (Θυοα)[32] and it is considered as the Mystery *par excellence.* The mass is an initiation (μυσταγωγία)[33] and this expression has continued to exist in the Greek Church to indicate the part of the ceremony in which the suffering of Christ is expressed.[34] It is basically the language of the Mysteries rather than that of the Gospel.

It could be thought that it is a matter of simple metaphor, and that is probably also the significance of the expressions used by the Apostle Paul. His 'Mystery', in The Revelation, is openly preached to all; his 'initiate' refers to all Christians. That is no longer the case, however, when we come to the documents of the third and fourth centuries where we shall see that the religion has assumed the ideas, without the original vocabulary.[35]

Distinction between Catechumens and Believers

It is superfluous to point out that such a distinction did not exist in apostolic times. The Acts abundantly prove that Jews and pagans did not have to pass through any trial period before declaring themselves to be converted by the preaching of the Gospel—no sooner converted than baptized.[36] But from the second century onwards, the Christians themselves were divided into two orders or classes, distinguished by baptism. Origen writes:

> The Christians address various admonitions to those who wish to become their disciples before accepting them in their midst. The purpose of these warnings is to strengthen the candidates in their resolve to lead a good life; they finally admit them when they see that they are in the state of mind desired and combine them in a separate Order (ἴδιον τάγμα). There are two Orders: one consisting of the newly initiated, who have not yet received their symbol of purity; the other of those who have given all possible proof of their resolve never to be unfaithful to the creed of Christianity.[37]

Tertullian even points to the absence of this distinction amongst the followers of certain sects as a sign of heresy: 'One does not know which of them is a catechumen and which a believer. As soon as they are listeners, they take part in the prayers and their apprentices are perfect before they have completed their instruction.'[38] Here we have a triple division: listeners; apprentices; and believers. It is no less clearly demonstrated in various parts of the *Apostolic Constitutions*.[39]

From a being a listener one became an apprentice by submitting to the instructions of a special ceremony. This had something of a first initiation which consisted of:

1. Blowing away the devil, accompanied or followed by incarnations.
2. Making the sign of the cross on the forehead.[40]

In the same way, those who wished to attain full initiation at Eleusis first had to pass through the Small Mysteries which consisted principally of purification ceremonies. I have already explained that these ceremonies in Antiquity invariably formed the preparation for the initiations.[41] The comparison has naturally had to intrude on the Greek Fathers of the Church, for we see them giving the deacons, responsible for exorcising the Devil, the title of 'Cathartists' (καθαρτικοι), which immediately recalls the expression καραρσις given to this part of the Mysteries. A part of Cyril's *Catechism* supposes that the neophyte stands with his head veiled while the incantations are recited.[42] Is this not the scene painted on an antique vase in which the neophyte can be seen sitting on a seat with his head veiled while the priestess waves the mystical fan above his head?

The apprentices occupied a special place near the entrance to the church and were present at the part of the service called 'the apprentices' mass'. It consisted of songs, prayers, preaching and reading.[43] One could remain an apprentice for one's entire life. Those who wished to become believers, had to undergo another initiation. In the same way, the initiates in the Small Mysteries who wished to be admitted to the Great Mysteries had to submit first to a new series of tests and purifications. The resemblance even struck the Fathers of the Church, Clement of Alexandria for example, who made the strongest attacks on the pagan Mysteries.[44]

The Rule of the Secret

I have already established that, according to the evidence of the Acts of the Apostles, neither the doctrine nor the ceremonies of the early communities were in any way secret. The situation is the same in the *Didache;* this restricts itself to recommending that the Eucharist should not be given to the unbaptized, 'because the Lord has said of it: Do not give what is sacred to the dogs.'[45] Towards the middle of the second century, Justin the Martyr still describes without hesitation the celebration of baptism and communion in the Apology which he directs to Antonius the Holy, i.e. to a pagan Emperor.[46] But at the beginning of the third century, Tertullian and Origen state the existence of ceremonies and formulas which it is forbidden to impart to the uninitiated.[47] Tertullian, Origen and Basil do not hesitate to justify this ban by referring to the example of the pagan Mysteries. Celsus had reproached the Christians with it. Origen state the existence of ceremonies and formulas which it is sophical sects which have external dogma and some other doctrine which is less laid bare to the eyes of all. . . . But in all the Mysteries, whether Greek or barbarian, no fault was found in keeping the secret.[48]

It frequently happens that when Origen and his successors in Christian preaching speak on problems concerning the sacraments, they suddenly break off to cry out, 'The Initiates know what I mean!' This is literally the same formula used by Pausanias, Plutarch and Apulaeus when they touch upon subjects monopolized by the Mysteries.

This esoteric part of Christianity included not only the celebration of baptism and communion[49] but also the sacramental formulas such as the words of the Pater and the Credo. These symbols had to be learned by heart and recited. The text is not even found in the *Catechism* in which Cyril explains the table of prayers for mass to the newly baptized. 'Take care', he writes, 'that you do not make these things known, not because they are unworthy of being repeated, but because profane ears are not worthy of hearing them.[50]

Likewise, Sozomenus refrains from mentioning the symbol of Nicaea in his Church history 'because the book may fall into the hands of the uninitiated.'[51]

In the Churches of the East, the altar and sometimes the *absida* were concealed by a curtain which was drawn across after the departure of the apprentices.[52] The latter had to retire when the acting priest spoke this formula: 'The sacred affairs for the Sacred'. A deacon then stepped forward saying, 'No apprentice, listener, unbeliever or heretic should remain. Those of them who took part in the first prayers should now leave. The mothers must take their children!' Replace the words 'unbeliever', 'listener' and 'apprentice' by 'ungodly', 'Epicurean', 'Christian' and you have the formula with which Alexander the Paphlagonian opened the Mysteries.[53] We have seen that at the beginning of the Great Mysteries, the Hierophant of Eleusis pronounced in similar terms the exclusion of those who knew no understandable language or were not pure. According to the apostolic laws, the deacon still had to ask, 'No one should remain if he is at variance with another or if he is contaminated with hypocrisy!' (ἐν υποκρίσει).[54]

The Degrees of Christian Initiation

The different episodes of initiation into the Christian Mysteries are summed up in the remarkable and important section in which Tertullian describes the spiritual powers of these acts. He writes, 'The body is bathed so that the soul may be cleansed of its impurities; the body is anointed so that the soul may be consecrated; the body is furnished with the sign of the cross so that the soul may be strengthened; the body is shaded by the laying-on of hands so that the soul may be enlightened by the Spirit; the body is fed with the flesh and blood of Christ so that the soul may sate itself with God.'[56] Here we have baptism, anointing, the sign of the cross, the laying-on of hands and the communion in the order in which these sacraments followed each other.

I have recalled that in the time of the Apostles baptism directly followed conversion. The ritual was extremely simple. The neophyte was immersed in the water of a lake or a river; a member of the community pronounced the following formula over him: 'I baptize you in the name of Jesus Christ'[57] or, 'I baptize you in the name of the Father, the Son and the Holy Ghost'.[58] Then one of the elders laid his hands upon him. At the time when the *Didache* was written, there appears to have been no requirement for the intervention of a special priest. 'He who baptizes' (ὁ βαπτίζιον) appears to allude to any given member of the community.[59] Mention begins to be made of preparatory moral instruction, but without regulating it; it is limited to prescribing a fast before the ceremony.[60] From the time of Justin the Martyr, baptism is described by expressions borrowed from pagan initiations (σφραγις, φωτισμος, μυστήριον); it is shortly to be solemnized no more than once a year. Sometimes, as in the well known cases of Constantia and Constantine, it will be postponed until the end of life. This arises because baptism is no longer the condition of admittance into the ranks of Christian society, but has become the reward of initiation into a higher degree of the Mysteries.

The apprentices who competed for this new initiation formed the group of the Chosen or the Competent (*φωὺζομενοὶ*, 'those who are enlightened'). They first had to submit to a whole series of doctrines and exercises which took place during the fasts. These meetings were called 'ballots', either because the neophytes were submitted to new trials, or because the believers were called on to express an opinion as to whether the candidates should be admitted or not. This is how the first ballot took place according to the manuscript 'The Wandering of Sylvia',[61] which described Christian religious practices in Jerusalem at the end of the fourth century. The bishop asked the neighbours of each candidate, 'Is he of good morals? Is he obedient to his parents? Is he not immoderate or vain?' The bishop then wrote down the names of those who had received a favourable testimony and sent all the others away while adding 'He should better himself and when he has bettered himself he should come and be baptized.' The foreigner who could find no witness was not easily admitted.[62] Is this not again the first session of the Great Mysteries, where, before the enrolment of the candidates, the Hierophant ordered anyone who did not possess the requisite moral conditions to withdraw?

Here again it is Origen who points out the resemblance when he quotes this sentence of Celsus: 'When the Mysteries of other religions are celebrated, only those will be initiated who have clean hands and a modest tongue or those who are free from all crime, whose soul is not tormented by remorse, who have always lived a good and honest life.[63]

Immediately following the enrolment, the purifications and the adjurations began which, in Rome, were sustained throughout seven meetings.[64] (We have seen that in Athens they took up the first three days of the Greek Mysteries.) In the last but one session, came the 'tradition' of the symbol. In the Roman ritual, this ceremony bore the significant name of 'opening of the ears'.[65] The last session took place the day before Easter—the day laid down for baptism. They passed on to the surrender of the symbol, whereby the candidate had to prove that he knew the text of the Credo by heart.[66]

The Roman Sacramentarians next show us the Chosen Ones who form a procession which, led by the Pope and his servants, goes to the baptistry while chanting litanies. Preceded by two deacons, each of whom is carrying a long candle, the procession enters the building which is bathed in a sea of light. The Pope consecrates the water in the basin by blowing over the surface making a sign of the cross over it and pouring in consecrated oil; the deacons then dip their burning candles in the water. The purpose of the latter action is clearly indicated in the *Missale Romanum,* which is still in force today, during the service on Holy Saturday when the priest, who dips an Easter candle, lit three times with a flint, in the baptismal font, says, 'That it may fully impregnate this water with its power.'[67] Among the Greeks, the purifying effect of the water was often heightened by dipping in pieces of firewood or torches which had been lit from the altar flame. In this manner the purifying effect of fire was added to that of water.[68] The blowing represents the third method of purifying which we have seen in use in classical paganism. The baptismal water therefore contained the three principal elements through which the candidate for the Mysteries formerly had to pass.

It would naturally be folly to claim that the Christians borrowed the oldest of their ceremonies from Greece.[69] But it is no less true that the similar use of the purifying bath had heightened the *rapprochement* with the Mysteries and facilitated the adoption of supplementary ceremonies which were completely foreign to the original Christianity, such as purification by oil and fire. 'It is not without reason', states Clement of Alexandria, 'that purification has the principal place in the Mysteries which are held in Greece.'[70] Fasting, which precedes baptism and communion, is another point of similarity with the ceremonies of Eleusis.

Meanwhile, the neophytes, turning to the West, the region of darkness, repeat the formula in which they renounce Satan. Following this, they turn to the East, the place of light. They are undressed and led to the basin. After asking them three questions in which the Credo is summed up, and having received the answers, the bishop repeats the baptismal formula over them. Immediately afterwards they come out of the water and, having put on a white garment, their heads are anointed. They are then taken to the signatorium, where the high priest makes the sign of the cross on their foreheads with his thumb which he has previously dipped in consecrated oil. From that moment on, they are 'sealed'. We do not know if the Mystics or Epopts at Eleusis were marked with a sign;

but the ceremony existed in other Mysteries, such as those of Mithras,[71] with the purpose either of indicating that the initiates had been through certain texts, or that they belonged to a new master. The procession is formed again and returns to the Basilica. Each initiate would carry a candle. In Alexandrian liturgy, he also wears a crown.[72]

It is precisely the Eleusinian procession where the Mystics, dressed in white, wearing a crown on their heads and carrying a torch in their hands, as may be seen on the bas-relief by Spon, pass by singing hymns on their way to the sanctuary. The Basilica is bathed in a sea of light; the image of Christ can be seen in this radiant light surrounded by angels. The descriptions of Chrysostamos, Cyril, the Pseudo Areopagite vie here with those of Claudius, Themistius and Plutarch who show us the gates of the telesterion when they are opened as hymns are sung, revealing the deity in a halo of heavenly light. The ceremony proceeded with the serving of mass in which the initiates partook of communion from a chalice which did not contain wine but the cyceon of the Eleusinian communion, a mixture of water, milk and honey which, according to an ancient writer, would make them understand that they have entered the Promised Land.[73] The service lasted until the first glimmer of dawn. As evening fell, they came to the Basilica again for Vespers, after which the new initiates were taken round the principal churches in the town. Sylvia informs us that in Jerusalem this trip included the Mount of Olives, Gethsemane, the Scourging Post, Golgotha, in fact all the places known from the Passion of Christ.[74] This pilgrimage, which was represented several times during Easter week, recalls a similar custom which we have noted during the sacred Wakes of Eleusis on the eve of the *dies lampadum,* when the Mystics visited the principal sanctuaries of the city and the places which played a role in the legend of Demeter.[75]

It goes without saying that this adoption of the form must exercise an influence on the content. Henceforth, it is no longer only the Gnostics who attribute an inner and, so to speak, mechanical influence to what for the writer of the First Letter to Paul is still simply a symbol of moral purification.[76] Tertullian and Irenaeus consider baptism to have truly magical power which itself brings about the forgiveness of sins, irrespective of the moral condition. For others, on the other hand, such as Clement of Alexandria, Gregory of Nazianza, Brazilaeus, Hieronymus, this remission demands belief and contrition as indispensable conditions. It is the old issue as to whether the robber Paetacion is saved because he has received initiation at Eleusis: the necessity for moral renewal will be admitted but it will also be explained that the ceremony is indispensable if one is to attain bliss. Hermas has the Apostles descending into the Scheol to baptize the patriarchs and the righteous of the Old Testament.[77] Clement of Alexandria, with his broad Neo-Platonic spirit, has them also baptizing pagans who are worth saving.[78]

Christian Symbolism

From its very origin, Christianity had a tendency to use figurative language, and consequently symbols. That is one of the features which contribute most to the originality and freshness of the Gospel. But these images have the purpose, as may be seen in the parables, of making the idea clearer and more attractive. The symbolism of the pagan Mysteries had, on the contrary, the dual aim of embodying certain instruction which remained hidden from the profane, and providing the initiates with a means of recognizing each other, only known to them. This kind of symbol included the painting which, according to the author of the *Philosophumena*, decorated the tabernacle of Phylya in the sanctuary of the Great Goddess and on which 'the image of all explained doctrine' was painted,[79] and the ear of corn which the Hierophant of Eleusis showed in utter silence in the Epopta. Similarly the *tesseres* were objects on which symbols were engraved and which the initiates took with them after their initiation, and which, accordingly to Apulaeus, embodied the sacred tradition.[80] All these uses of symbolism are discovered in the early communities which were established on pagan territory; for example the art of the catacombs.[81]

Christ is represented by the Good Shepherd or even by Orpheus, the wise man whom the author of *Philosophumena* calls, 'he who was the pre-eminent revealer of initiation and Mysteries'.[82] The immortality of the soul was represented by the lovely image of Psyche, paradise by a grape-vine and small-winged spirits. Most of the allegories were, as was to be expected, borrowed from the Old Testament and Gospel tradition: the Resurrection was represented by Jonah who came out of the whale or Lazarus arising from the grave or Elias who ascended to heaven in a chariot.[83]

The cross is seen or concealed in the most varied images: anchor, trident, mast etc. The allusion to baptism and communion are very indirect: Moses bringing forth water from a rock with his staff; a fisherman casting his line into the water; the cripple who comes out of the bath and carries his sick bed on his head; the sacrifices of Abraham; a table with bread and a fish; the seven baskets of the miracle of the multiplication of the loaves, etc.

The symbol, *par excellence,* which also gave the password and the symbol of recognition is the secret name of Jesus Christ, Son of God, Saviour (*ἰχθύς*).[84] The image of a fish was engraved on ring stones, lamps, gravestones etc. There were also metal or ivory pictures in the shape of a fish which were able to play a similar role to that of the countermarks discovered in the vicinity of Eleusis—these bore a symbol related to the Mysteries.[85] The symbolism of the fish does not appear to be older than the end of the second century, i.e. the time when the Christian religion assumed the form of a Mystery.[86] The Greeks applied the expression 'symbol' not only to the signs and images, but also to the sacramental formulas which were known exclusively to the initiates. Thus, the symbols of the Mysteries had a double significance, i.e. while they had a literal meaning, they also had a second, hidden significance. On the other hand, the meaning of the Christian symbol was openly expressed. But the very use of the word 'symbol' reflected the spirit of the Mysteries.[87]

The *Traditio Symboli* was not limited to imparting the Credo; it also contained the text of the Paternoster and, in Rome, those of other important Christian documents. Furthermore, all the Gospels were brought before the eyes of the neophytes. Four deacons brought them ceremoniously into the vestry and laid them in turn on the four corners of the altar. If the communication of the holy objects during mass is added, one can again find the similarity with the *παραδόσις των ἱερῶν*, where the Hierophant of Eleusis exhibited the *hiera* to the initiates and taught them the mystical formulas for which he undoubtedly gave some explanation.[88]

The Ritual of Mass

I must still speak about the actual mass, or rather the communion which formed the central point of it and which, more than baptism, was the Mystery *par excellence.* In Eleusis there were originally two kinds of ceremony: those with the aim of introducing the neophyte to mystical life and those which had to enable him to realize the purpose of the Mysteries. They later flowed together, but some difference must always have remained between the ceremonies in which the followers took part once, at the time of initiation, and those in which they participated every time they celebrated the Mysteries.[89]

It is superfluous to recall here that the communion was in Apostolic times a communal meal with the dual purpose of remembering the last supper of Jesus and establishing the existence of a consubstantial link both between the participants themselves and with their master. The *Didache* merely mentions the thanksgiving formulas which had to be repeated to consecrate to God the bread and wine of which each believer brought his share.[90]

The meal was gradually separated from the Eucharist and eventually given up altogether. I really do not need to pursue here the development of communion from the doctrinaire point of view. The only points from it which I should like to recall are the following:

1. By the third century the Holy Sacrament had become a sacrifice, the efficacy of which depended on the formulas repeated by the priest himself, who is shown as the sacrificer *par excellence.*
2. Whilst for some, such as Clement of Alexandria, it remained a mystical symbol, for others it became a realistic and magical act, with the purpose of ensuring eternal life; a magic potion for immortality (*φάρμακον ἀθανσίας*).
3. It is generally held to be a Mystery, not only in the sense that its fundamental idea may go above human understanding, but also in that it is a ceremony, the sight or knowledge of which must be kept hidden from the uninitiated.
4. It has become encircled by ceremonies which take us back to the Mysteries of the Greeks, and particularly to Eleusis.

These ceremonies form the main part of the mass which was celebrated behind closed doors after the apprentices have left. Not only the Last Supper is symbolically recalled by it but also the suffering, the death and the resurrection of Christ. A parallel can be drawn here too with the ceremonies of the Epopta where the suffering of a God is represented in ceremonies, the celebration of which ensured the participants' bliss in the life hereafter. As far as I know, the gods of the pagan Mysteries, Dionysus, Cora, Attis, Adonis and Osiris were never represented as having *voluntarily* undergone suffering and death to ensure the salvation of the believers. But by their suffering and their resurrection these gods filled no less the role of Saviour which we find in the concept of the Christian Messiah. Even in the consuming of divine flesh and blood to provide the happiness of a higher life, a coarse resemblance is found in the ceremony of omophagia which is described by a writer belonging to Protestant orthodoxy as 'a mythological Eucharist'.[91]

According to the Sacramentarians, mass begins with prayers for the Church, the bishop and his priests, the emperor, the sick, the poor, travellers, even for heretics, Jews and pagans. In Eleusis, the Great Mysteries also began with sacrifices 'for the Senate and the people, for the well-being of women and children'.[92] At the end of these prayers, the bishop, helped by his priests, goes to receive the gifts of bread, wine and oil which have been brought by the believers. In Eleusis, they likewise offered the first-fruits of the harvest, either in sheaves or in the form of biscuits. The Archdeacon selects from the gifts the bread to be used for communion and arranges it on the altar next to the chalice which he fills. In Eastern liturgy where gifts from the people died out early on, these preparations were made with prayers and special ceremonies before the solemn entrance of the serving priest. It is as though an attempt has been made here to graft one Mystery onto another.[93] This ceremony, really the most important of the entire mass, was solemnized at a special altar, the πρόθεσυς, out of sight of the believers; only the priests could be present. When the ceremony was over, the sacred objects, i.e. the chalice, the paten and the tabernacle which contained the bread, were wrapped in three cloths of linen, silk, and gold and then carried in procession to the high altar while the choir began to sing a *keroubicon* or a *halleluja*.[94] One may recall,[95] that the *hiera* intended for the celebration of the Mystery, were solemnly taken from Athens to Eleusis, hidden from all eyes.

Then followed the recitation of the Canon in which the serving priest explained the origin and the significance of the communion, just as the mystical drama explained the institution and significance of the ceremonies established by Demeter. At this moment in the Roman liturgy, the blessing of the beans takes place; on August 6th that of the grapes and on Maundy Thursday, that of oil intended for the sick.[96] Only then is the communion begun. At the end of this, the priest repeats the prayers of thanksgiving after which he dismisses those present with the phrase, 'Ite, missa est', just as the Hierophant announced the end of the Mysteries by the still unexplained formula, 'Conx ompax', and the high priest of the Isis-cult sent his audience away with, Λαοτς ἄφεσις.[97]

It can still be demonstrated how the Mysteries influenced the development of priestly thought. In the fourth century we are far from the time when all Christians were called priests. The priest is henceforth the Hierophant who alone can celebrate the sacrifice because he alone knows the secret of the Mysteries. The Pseudo Areopagite wrote this remarkable sentence in connection with the commmunion: 'There, where the majority bow down to see purely divine symbols, the archpriest, under the inspiration of the Divine Spirit, is brought, in the manner of a high priest, to reveal in blissful, spiritual contemplation the sacred reality of the Mysteries.' One cannot help thinking here of what I have already quoted from Theodoret:[98] 'All do not know what the Hierophant knows, the majority only see what is represented. Those who are called priests fulfil the ceremonies of the Mysteries; the Hierophant alone knows the reasons for what he does and he imparts this to whoever he finds worthy.'[99]

The sacrifice of mass gradually assumed the character of adjuration and penance. It was celebrated to put an end to drought or cattle sickness, to ensure a fertile harvest—thus returning to the original purpose of the Eleusinian Mysteries.

Cause and Fate of Christian Esotericism

All these points of contact with pagan institutions could not fail to amaze and annoy the Christians who had to wage war against the last defenders of paganism. There were two explanations available to clarify this resemblance: it was either a weakened, corrupt echo among the unbelievers of the revelations which were handed down intact through former centuries to the Christians; or it was a stroke of the Devil who did all in his power to ridicule the true faith. 'Habet ergo diabolus Christos tuos', says Firmicus Maternus with reference to the resurrection of Dionysus in the Mysteries.[100]

Nowadays, less fantastic explanations are given, but that does not mean that they are resting on safer ground. We have pointed out the necessity for the first Christians to hide their religion from their persecutors. But the disciplinary rule of secrecy in this respect did more harm than good, as we can see in the refutation of Celsus by Origen. It sanctioned all possible charges without hiding the fact of Christianity.

There has also been speculation on the wish to make converts by the attraction of secret revelations. Alexander of Abonoteichos would smile at such an assessment; it absolutely contradicts what we know of the simplicity and earnestness of the early Christian communities.

Hatch appears to come nearer to the truth when he attributes this change to the influence of the converted who had left paganism and took with them the form of worship to which they were accustomed.[101] On the other hand, the Mysteries, as Harnack quite rightly remarks, had become in Greek society an indispensable institution.[102] All foreign religions had to assume the same form, whether they came from Egypt or Syria, Chaldea or Persia. But these conscious or unconscious links with the forms of the past could not have induced Christian priests to use pagan ceremonies if the latter, as I have demonstrated at the beginning of the chapter, had not broken every link with the worship of certain gods. They were henceforth merely symbols, forms of organization or of worship for the use of any faith. Why then should the Greek Christian communities have felt any objection to accepting their introduction?

Christian esotericism flourished for a short time only. After continuing until the beginning of the sixth century, it suddenly vanished, almost without any discussion, while changes relating to merely subordinate points of dogma, discipline and liturgy provoked endless discussion and serious ruptures. The group of apprentices considerably shrank as the number of pagans grew less and the custom of child baptism became more generalized. The ritual of Constantinople has to this day retained the formula of dismissal of apprentices, but the Roman ritual of the eighth century no longer bore any trace of it. At the end of the sixth century, the gallican liturgy still contained this formula, 'juxta anticum Ecclesiae ritum'. But when it then commands the doors to be guarded, to prevent the entry of the profane, St Germain of Paris explains this as an allusion to the doors of the soul![103] The handing down and the passing on of the symbol was transferred to the instruction given to children for their first communion. The

Eucharist became a public ceremony. The places of worship were open to everyone, and if today there remain any traces of the esotericism which for more than three centuries seemed to be one of the principal elements of the Church, then it is, in the Greek Church, the presence of the iconostasis which lies between the people and the priests and in the Latin Church, the use of a dead language, the custom of saying 'Our Father' quietly during the service and the prohibition on reading the Scriptures in the vernacular.

However, the ceremonies borrowed from the Old Mysteries did not totally disappear with the rules of discipline of secrecy which contributed so much to bringing them into the Church. There are some which are still celebrated under our very eyes, and in this respect one could find no better words than those of the Anglican theologian whose investigations have contributed so much to revealing the link between Christianity and the doctrine and worship of Hellenism. Hatch writes:

> In the brilliant ceremonial of the Greek and Latin Churches, in the splendour of the lights, in the isolation of the central rite, in the procession of the torch-bearers chanting hymns, we find the survival, and sometimes the artificial survival, of what I have not the heart to call a pagan ceremony; for, although it was the expression of a less enlightened faith, it was, however, no less an offering to the deity, by a soul just as earnest as ours in its searching for God and its aspiration to holiness.

The unbroken line of religions, however antipathetic it may be to certain theologians, remains the best evidence that religion has its roots in human nature and that its development follows a general law of progress.

[1]Apulaeus, *Metamorph.* 1, XI, 23.

[2]Garruci, 'Les Mystères du syncrétisme phrygien', in the 4th part of the *Melanges d'Archéologie* by Cahier and Martin, p. 1 and following.

[3]Lenormant, *Revue de l'Architecture* (paris, 1868), p. 59.

[4]Eunapus, *Vit. Maxim.* (Didot), p. 476.

[5]Harnack, *Précis de l'Histoire des Dogmas,* translation by Choisy (Paris, 1893).

[6]E. Hatch, 'Influence of Greek Ideas and Usages upon the Christian Church', Hibbert Lectures (London, 1890).

[7]G. Anrich, *Das antike Mysterienwesen in seinem Einfluss auf das Christentum* (Göttingen, 1894). Also: G. Wobermin, *Frage der Beeinflussung des Urchristentums durch das antike Mysterienwesen* (Berlin, 1896).

[8]F. Vopiscus, *Vita Saturnini,* 8.

[9]See what the writer of the *Philosophumena* says of the Naasseners (V, I, Cruice,

Paris, 1860, p. 176 and following). See also Irenaeus, *Contra Haereses,* I, 23, with reference to Simon Magus (Migne, p. 671 and following).

[10]M. Wobbermin refers to Gnosticism as Christian Orphism.

[11]*Philosophumena,* lib. I.

[12]Origen, *Contra Celsum,* Book VI, p. 649 (Migne). This drawing has been reconstructed by Matter according to the information of Origen. (*Histoire Critique du Gnosticisme,* Paris, 1843, ch. 17.)

[13]Amélineau, *Gnosticisme égyptien,* p. 243 and following. Amélineau later gave a French translation of the *Pistis Sophia* (Paris, 1895).

[14]Eugène de Faye, 'Introd. à l'histoire du gnosticisme' in the *Revue de l'Hist. des Rel.,* part XLVI (1902), p. 396. See Edwin Hatch, *Influence of Greek Ideas and Usages upon the Christian Church,* p. 305 and following.

[15]Irenaeus, *Contra Haereses,* I, 23 (migne), p. 673.

[16]'Extracts Theodot', No. 64, in Amélineau, *Gnosticisme égyptien,* p. 228.

[17]Irenaeus, *Contra Haereses,* I. 21, 3 (Migne), p. 662.

[18]This expression *νυμφών* was also applied to a temple at Phlya, dedicated to Dionysus, Demeter and Cora (Pausanias II, 11, 3).

[19]Tertullian, 'Eleusinia Valentine fecerunt lenocinia' (*Advers. Valentian,* Paris, 1634, p. 289).

[20]Matter, *Hist. Critique du Gnosticisme,* part I, p. 378.

[21]See the texts collected by Fr. Lenormant in his *Monographie de la Voie Sacrée Eleusinienne* (Paris, 1864), part I, p. 52.

[22]*Philosophumena* 1, V, 3, Cruice, p. 219.

[23]*οἰ πνευματικοὶ ἅνωθεν ἀπο του* 'Αοάμαντος *ῥυέντες κατω* in *Philosophumena,* V, 1 (Cruice, p. 171).

[24]Epiphan, *Panarium Adv. Ophet.,* lib. I, 5 (Migne), p. 272).

[25]Proclus, *Commentaire de Timée,* II, 130.

[26]See text and translation in the thesis of Paul Sabatier? *La Didache ou l'Enseignement des Douze Apôtres* (Paris, 1885). Sabatier attributes a much greater age to this document; he places it in apostolic times, even in the middle of the first century. It is certain that Christianity from the *Didache* has nothing dogmatic nor churchlike about it; the only critierion is morality.

[27]L. Duchesne, *Orig. du culte chrétien,* 2nd edn. (Paris, 1898).

[28]Principally Emile Burnouf, in his *Science des Religions* (Paris, 1876), p. 92 and following.

[29]The writer does not appear to know that even today very many theosophists support this theory. (Editor of Dutch edition.) ''Αγιος *γίνομαι μυούμενος ιεροφαντει δὲ ὄ κύριος και τὸν μυοτήν σφραγίζεται φωταγωγων.* *Prototeptique,* XII, 120.

[30]See for this terminology the references in the works mentioned above and especially Hatch (*Greek Influence,* pp. 295-298).

[31]Basil, *De spirit. Sanct.,* XXVII (Paris, 1730), part III, p. 55; Sozomène, *Hist. Eccles.* I, 20 (Cambridge), p. 39.

[32]*Apostol. Constit.,* in Mansi, *Consilia* (1759), part I, lib II.

[33]Cyril, *Hierosol., Catech. Mystag.* I (Oxford, 1703), p. 277.

[34]'Rituale Graecum' in Maury, *Rel. de la Grèce Antique,* part II, p. 301.

[35]For the expressions *σωραγὶs οφραγιξειν, φωτισμοs, ρωτίζειν* see Wobbermin, pp. 143-145. Wobbermin also finds in Orphism the precursors of the expressions *όμοοίνοs* and *μονογενήs.*

[36]Acts 2:38, 41; 8:12, 13, 36-38; 10:47-48; 16:15, 33; 18:8; 19:5.

[37]Origen, *Contra Celsum,* lib. III, 481 (Migne).

[38]'Ante sunt perfecti quam edocti'. Tert. *De Praescr. Haeret.,* XVI. (Opera, Paris, 1630), p. 95.

[39]*Apostol. Constit.,* lib. VIII, ch. VI-XIII.

[40]Duchesne, *Origines du culte chrétien,* p. 285 etc.

[41]See the article by Lustatio van Bouché-Leclercq in the *Dict. of Daremberg and Saglio.* He writes, 'the mystical religious practices were true purification ceremonies from which one issued fully prepared to undertake the journey to the other side of the grave, absolved of sin, signed with the seal (σωϱαγίs) of the Chosen Ones and ensured of the benevolence of the gods of the Underworld.' (*Fascic.* 31, p. 1424, col. 1).

[42]'Εσκέπασπᾶι σον τὸ πϱόσωπον. Cyril, *Hierosol. Praefat. Catech.* (Oxford, 1703), p. 7.

[43]Duchesne points out that this whole section of the Christian religious practice has been borrowed from the synagogue. Origen, p. 59.

[44]*Stromat.* V, 4.

[45]*Didache* IX, 5.

[46]Just. the Martyr, *Apolog.* I, ch. 61 (Jena), p. 257 etc.

[47]Mgr P. Batiffol has published a book titled *Etudes d'histoire et de théologie positive* (Paris, 1902), in which he maintains that the rule of the Arcanum was never a church law, but simply an apprentices' rule, the significance of which has been exaggerated. Indeed, it was not formulated by any council.

In a criticism which is rather strong, not withstanding its courtesy, Mr van Hove, Professor in Church History at the University of Leuven, replies (*Bulletin Bibliographique du Musée Belge,* April, 1903), 'Let us not argue over words. Can a custom have no legal power? What council established apprenticeship and so many other points of Church discipline?'

[48]*Contra Celsum,* lib. I, 326 (Migne).

[49]'What do we have which is secret and not public?' writes Augustine. 'The sacraments of baptism and communion.' (*Psalmum,* C., III).

[50]Cyril, *Hierosol. Praefat. Catech.,* VII, p. 10.

[51]οὐ γὰϱ ἄπειχος και των ὀ μὐητων τινχs τῆδἐ τη Βίβλὼ ἑντυχειν. *Histor. Eccles.,* ch. 20 (Cambridge), p. 39.

[52]'The veil', writes Mgr Duchesne, 'is still used in Eastern ceremonies; it is hung over the middle door of the iconotasis; it is opened and closed at given moments in the ancient liturgy.'. (*Orig. du culte chrétien,* p. 79).

[53]*Apostolic. Constit.,* lib. VIII, ch. 12. The Latin formula was, 'Si quis catechumena est, recedat.'

[54]Lucian, *Alexand.,* 38.

[55]*Apost. Const.,* VIII, 12. See *Didache,* XIV, 2.

[56]Tertullian, *De Resurrect. Carnis,* ch. 8 (Opera, 1630), part II, p. 553.

[57]The Acts 2:38; 8:16; 10:48.

[58]*Math.,* 28:19.

[59]*Didache,* VII, 3.

[60]*Ibid.*

[61]The Latin text is given as an appendix in the work of Mgr Duchesne, *Origines du culte chrétien,* p. 472 and following. This Sylvia came from Gaul; according to

some writers she was the sister of the famous Rufinus.

[62]Peregrin, 'Silviae', in Duchesne, *Orig. du culte chr.*, p. 499.

[63]Origen, *Contra Celsum,* lib. III (Migne), p. 486.

[64]The Mysteries of Mithras have seven degrees of trials which the neophytes must undergo. Perhaps the different ballots would have developed to the same consecutive number if the evolution of the Christian liturgy had not ceased to move in this direction.

[65]Duchesne, *Orig.*, p. 286 and following.

[66]In the Syrian Church, this was not yet the end. The candidates were invited to descend into the Crypt of the Holy Tomb to receive the communication of a 'higher' Mystery, which was the baptismal formula itself: 'Verba quae sunt mysterii alterioris, id est ipsius baptismi quae adhuc catechumeni audire non polestis.' Peregrin, 'Silv.', in Duchesne, p. 500.

[67]*Missale Romanum* (Tournay, 1879), p. 270.

[68]Euripides, *Hercule Furieux,* line 928; Aristophanes, *Peace,* 959. See Bouché-Leclercq under the word 'Lustration' in the *Dict. Daremberg et Saglio,* part V, p. 140.

[69]Baptism was used by the Jews before the advent of Christ. Maimonides referred to it, along with circumcision, as the sign of acceptance of proselytes in Judaism. (Sebaties, *La Didache,* p. 85). From early Christianity onwards, it appears with the double character of purifying and enlightening which it also had in the Mysteries. The expression φωτισθέντες is already found in the Letter to the Hebrews 6:4.

[70]Clement of Alexandria, *Stromat.*, V, 4.

[71](Mithras) 'signat illic in frontibus milites suos.' Tertullian, *De Praescript. Haeretic.*, ch. 40 (Opera, Paris, 1630), part II, p. 92.

[72]E. Hatch, *Influence of Greek Ideas and Usages,* p. 298.

[73]In Hatch, *op. cit.*, p. 300. Porphyrus emphasizes that the honey has both purifying and prophylactic properties, Καὶ καταρθικήσεστι δυνάμεω και συντηρηνκης. *De Antro Nymph.*, XV.

[74]Duchesne, p. 486 and following.

[75]The features of baptism were more or less the same in the Churches of the East, except that the renunciation of Satan took place in the forecourt of the baptistry and before the neophytes descended into the basin they were anointed from head to toe. (Cyril, *Hierosol. Catech. Mystag.*, II, 4, 285-286).

[76]I Peter 3:21: 'The like figure whereunto even baptism doth also now save us (not the putting away of the filth of the flesh, but the answer of a good conscience toward God).'

[77]Hermas Shepherd, *Similt.*, IX, 16 (Leipzig, 1876), p. 233.

[78]Clement of Alexandria, *Stromat.*, II, 9; see VI, 6.

[79]Philosophumena V, 3. (Cruice), p. 218.

[80]Apulaeus, *Apol.* (Didot), p. 235.

[81]See the works of Rossi, *Roma Sotterranea Christiana, 3 parts, (1864-77). See also Ch. Roller, Les Catacombes de Rome,* 2 parts, (1881).

[82]*του τὰς τελετάς μαλιστα και τα μυστήρια κατα δειξαντος* 'Ορφεως. *Philos.*, V, 3. See Aristophanes, *Ranae,* 1032.

[83]Cumont has shown that this last theme is directly copied from the Mithraic representations of Helios who takes Mithras up in his chariot. (*Mysteries of Mithras,* I, p. 178).

[84]'The Christ,' says Origen, 'who is figuratively called the fish.' „Χριστός ὀτροπικῶς λεγομένος ἰχθυς. (*Comment. in Matth.,* XIII, Migne, 584). The Christians went so far as to call themselves 'sons of the Fish' (Hieronymus, *Epistle* 7, Migne, 339).

[85]*Bulletin et correspondance hellénique* (1884), pl. II.

[86]Roller, *Catacombes,* I, p. 107.

[87]Towards the fourth century, the symbol in Jerusalem had a double explanation, one literal, the other spiritual; at least that is claimed by the 'Wanderings of Sylvia'. ('Primum carnaliter et sie spiritualiter, ita et symbolum exponet.' In Duchesne, *Orig. du culte.,* p. 500).

[88]Mgr Duchesne believes a figurative representation of the *Traditio Symboli* can be found in a scene which frequently appears on Christian monuments in the Catacombs: Christ sitting on a throne on the top of a mountain from which four springs are flowing; around him the Apostles or other believers who are receiving a book on which is written 'Dominus dat legem'. Duchesne, *Orig. du culte chrét.,* p. 291.

[89]See *Chapter I.*

[90]See Harnack, *Précis,* pp. 15 and 67.

[91]E. de Pressensé, *l'Ancien Monde et le Christianisme* (Parish, 1887), p. 463.

[92]See Fr. Lenormant in *Daremberg et Saglio,* part II, 1st edn., p. 566.

[93]The formula used to consecrate the elements was secret. Basil notes that the words of the Eucharist invocation do not appear in the rites and dogma entrusted to paper, although they were of apostolic origin. *De Spiritu Sancto,* XXVII (Paris, 1730), part III, p. 55.

[94]Duchesne, *Origines du culte chrétien,* p. 78.

[95]See *Chapter I,* 'The Procession of Eleusis.'

[96]Duchesne, *Orig. du culte chrét.,* p. 175.

[97]Apulaeus, *Metamorph.,* XI, 17.

[98]Theodoret, *De Fide* (Paris, 1642), IV, p. 482.

[99]*Ibid.*

[100]*De Errore Prof. Relig.,* XXIII.

[101]Hatch, *Greek Influence,* p. 292.

[102]Harnack, *précis,* p. 15.

[103]Duchesne, *Orig. du culte chrét.,* p. 194.

INDEX